Catholic Living Series   *Vol. IX*

KEEPING YOUR BALANCE IN THE MODERN CHURCH

Hugh J. O'Connell, C.SS.R., Ph.D.

LIGUORIAN PAMPHLETS
REDEMPTORIST FATHERS
Liguori, Missouri 63057

Imprimi Potest:
Raymond Schmitt, C.SS.R.
Provincial, St. Louis Province
Redemptorist Fathers
August 1, 1968

Imprimatur:
St. Louis, August 3, 1968
✠ John J. Carberry
Archbishop of St. Louis

TABLE OF CONTENTS

UNIT I

UNIT II

UNIT I

CHAPTER I

NEW IDEAS NEED SIFTING

This is a book on the state of religion today. It's for the average intelligent Catholic. By this we mean anyone—layman, priest or nun—who is not a professional scholar.

We make no claim to instruct those who can pronounce "Schillebeeckx" without the quiver of an eyebrow, or who prop up one of Karl Rahner's more involved treatises behind their morning bowl of corn flakes and digest with equal facility both the corn flakes and the theology. Such persons can more than take care of themselves!

Our purpose is to explain how the present differences of opinion on many aspects of Catholic life began and developed before, during and after Vatican Council II.

Some of the ideas discussed may at first sound strange and difficult. This is because they involve new modes of thought and language with which Catholics are mostly unfamiliar. However, we will try to make things as clear and simple as possible. There is a very definite progression of ideas. If you stick with it, you will surely understand a great deal more about what has been going on in the Church.

Incidentally, this book is just as suitable for the ordinary Protestant. The basic religious questions he is confronted by today are much the same.

NO FAIR SHAKE

There is good reason to think that the average person has not been given a fair shake in this age of renewal. He has been thrown into the arena of religious controversy without adequate explanation of the issues involved, and without means of distinguishing between opinions that are solid and well-founded and those which are extreme, either on the right or on the left.

He is told that he has to be mature, make decisions for himself, doubt, probe and question. But he honestly realizes that he is not prepared by education or training to read and understand, let alone make decisions about the statements of authors who are arguing, for instance, about the "dehellenization" of Christianity.

As a result, he is bewildered and confused and, in many cases, anxious and fearful. Donald J. Thorman writes: "It seems to me that if labels are useful, the one I'd have to pin on today's laity is: The Uncertain Catholic. The characteristic note of today's American Catholic is confusion, indecision; we are treading water, waiting, wondering what is going to happen next. This is the age of the question mark. We no longer feel certain we have all the answers to all of men's problems. We are no longer certain if we know all the right questions" (America, Jan. 14, 1967, p. 39).

EVEN PRIESTS AND NUNS

Nor is this confusion and uncertainty confined to the laity. It has spread to some extent even among priests and nuns. Among these we are hearing of "crises of identity," reflected in such statements as: "I don't know what it means to be a priest"; "I don't know why I am a nun."

Although no exact and reliable figures are available, it certainly seems that more young men are leaving the priesthood and more Sisters are leaving the convent than before. At least, they are making a lot more noise about it. Back in the old days, for the most part, the departing priest or nun would slip quietly back into secular life. Now a good many think they have to make a speech about it, explaining and justifying their action. A few are even vitriolic in their attacks on what they call "the Institutional Church."

NEW AIR OF FREEDOM

A good many of the religious problems of the average Catholic laymen, priests and nuns, who make no claim to be specialists or scholars, stem from the new air of freedom of theological thought and discussion resulting from Vatican II. By no means is this meant to imply that such freedom of thought and discussion is bad, or that it should be stifled. If properly employed, it can bring a new wave of enthusiasm, of dedication to the cause of Christ, of dynamic effort to transform the world according to God's plan. It can shake us out of our lethargy, our contentment with the *status quo,* our indifference to the tremendous social evils that beset mankind.

That's why Pope John XXIII called for "an opening of the windows of the Church in order to let in fresh air." That is what Pope Paul VI meant when he said: "The spirit of the Council is fervor, awakening, alertness, good will, spiritual devotion, zeal—new prospects, new hopes, new activities—force and fire."

The great danger, as every reasonable man must recognize, is that freedom brings with it the possibility that it will be abused. In the days before Vatican II, there was actually a very considerable amount of theological speculation and innovation; there were battles quite as heated as those going on today. The only difference was that such ideas were quietly presented in theological journals, and were subjected by experts to analysis and investigation, to a weighing of reasons pro and con, to a more or less general acceptance or rejection by qualified theologians before they ever came to public attention.

Moreover, among Catholics the shock of new religious ideas on the minds of those who were not experts was cushioned by the censorship of books and articles and by the index of prohibited books. Before a book treating on religion could be published by a Catholic, it had to be submitted for censorship in order to obtain an *imprimatur*. If the book was considered to contain opinions contrary to Catholic doctrine, to the decrees of the Holy See, or even too wild and revolutionary, permission to print would be denied. To the liberal, who claimed the right to make up his own mind about religious truth, such censorship was intolerable. To the person who felt no competence to judge between truth and error in complex religious questions, it was a comfort.

SHIFT TOWARD FREEDOM

With the opening of Vatican II, the climate in the Church definitely shifted toward freedom of thought and expression in theological matters. This note was sounded by Pope John XXIII in his opening address to the bishops at the start of the Council. Pope John's characteristic optimism breaks through in almost every line of this address. He is confident that the Church will derive new energies and new strengths from the Council and that "she will look to the future without fear."

Although he recognizes that the work of the Council is to defend and to advance the course of apostolic truth, he leaves no doubt that in his mind the advance is the important thing. He chides those whom he called "prophets of doom," who are always forecasting disaster. The Church, he says, must never depart from the patrimony of truth received from the Fathers; nevertheless, "it must ever look to the present, to new conditions and forms of life introduced into the modern world, which have opened new avenues to the Catholic apostolate."

Although the pope recognized the need of guarding against fallacious teaching and dangerous concepts, he was not overly concerned about them. He declared: "It is evident that the truth of the Lord will remain forever. We see, in fact, as one age succeeds another, that the opinions of men follow one another and exclude each other. And often errors vanish as quickly as they arise, like fog before the sun.

"The Church has always opposed these errors. Frequently she has condemned them with the greatest severity. Nowadays, however, the Spouse of Christ prefers to make use of the medicine of mercy rather than that of severity. She considers that she meets the needs of the present day by demonstrating the validity of her teaching rather than by condemnations."

THE BURDEN IS ON YOU

The new freedom gives a tremendous opportunity for the circulation of fresh ideas, for the reformulation and restatement of ancient truths; but it also gives the opportunity, as Pope John himself declared, for the introduction and rapid circulation of false and erroneous opinions which are contrary to divinely revealed truths. This throws a burden on ordinary Catholics to sift what they read and hear about religious matters, a chore they were not required to do before. Here are some suggestions for this difficult task:

GUIDELINES

Obviously the most powerful means of news communication is the secular press, radio and TV. How is religious news handled by TV, or any of the loud voices in the field? It is fragmented, highlighted, taken out of context. This doesn't necessarily make it a lie. It is like any other news we get—not the full story. Simply must be a digest! Perhaps most of all, it must be geared to sell. This often means there is going to be more than a hint of sensationalism, of the spectacular.

Is there any reason why we should expect newsmen to report religious news differently than any other? Should we want them to? Good men though they be, any other attempt or aim would set them up as teachers, posts they neither want nor are qualified for. Should we then not be as ready to sift religious news coverage as any other?

How many times have you read of an event reported in a large secular magazine at home, and again in another publication at the doctor's office or somewhere else? If the event has any complexity at all, you will find different slants, different points of view, different quotations proving different things, different motives and prejudices. The writers don't claim, and we don't expect from them, infallibility. Fidel Castro, for instance, was enshrined on almost every magazine cover during the Cuban revolution. It was a mistake—but the reporters aren't God and the publications not the Bible. Your task is to weigh what you read, and to try to put an objective evaluation upon it.

If these principles were applied to religious news coverage in the secular press, much confusion would be eliminated.

However, the problem goes beyond the secular press. What about the Catholic press, which traditionally has had instruction and positive teaching as a goal? Even here, contradictory reporting, attitudes that clash with each other are undoubtedly causing confusion today.

Again some basic ideas may help us to be good sifters.

In the Church there has always been a continuing search for new insights into old truths, a constant delving into the message of our Lord for a more comprehensive understanding. Theology calls this the evolution of dogma.

From this basis the theologians, the "thinking mind of the Church," must proceed. What is to be thought of new medical procedures, they ask, in the light of Christ's teaching? What implications follow from the right of a man to own private property or from the relationship between unions and employers? Every new age brings new and different encounters. Not to evolve is to fossilize Christ in the pages of ancient history. It is forever to keep Him out of the very market place in which He came to teach.

THE PLACE OF OPINION

However the first step of such evolution is *opinion*. Individual, responsible men must have opinions which they air and share with other responsible men. Usually much time and debate are required before a legitimate conclusion can be reached. Can you imagine the number of individual opinions that have been put forth, thought over and shot down, never reaching the state of Church teaching! Should one be surprised at the numerous individual opinions circulating today? Not to have fresh ideas, new light with which to re-examine the teachings of Christ is to die; and to take opinion for Church teaching is equally fatal.

No matter how simple and easy things were in the past, no matter how much some may wish the good old days would return, they will not. Both the popes and the Council have called for the Church to undertake a process of self-examination, renewal and reform. To fulfill her divine mission, she must enter into dialogue with the modern world, try to understand its problems, speak its language, and exert her saving influence upon it.

The Church has this mission simply because this was and is the mission of Christ. This demands an involvement with the world today, a changed and changing world. Today's new technology, new orientation to life, has created a whole new environment that the Church must give witness to, rescue and serve. And though she speaks of ancient truths with her divine commission undimmed, she must speak in a way that modern man can understand.

This is why change has been called for. It is no favor to Christ to try to do today's job with yesterday's tools. But in a time of change, one must inevitably expect confusion and some irresponsible reporting and writing. If we only remember that this is a time of sifting, the confusion need not be so complete, the price to be paid not so high for a full understanding of the renewal Vatican II has called for.

SUMMARY

We might summarize what has been said in the following propositions:

1. Don't close your mind to new ideas and opinions; but don't accept uncritically everything you read and hear.

2. Be careful to distinguish what is merely opinion from the official teaching of the Church.

3. Try to weigh the reasons for opinions; don't accept them just because some well-known man is quoted as having stated them.

4. Try to get the whole picture, and not merely a distortion of the truth.

5. Be patient; we're going through a period of change, and it takes time to get things sorted out correctly.

6. Listen to the teaching authority of the Church, which alone, with the help of the Holy Spirit, can make the final judgment as to what is, or is not, divinely revealed truth.

Discussion Points

1. Many speak of today's "confused and uncertain Catholics." How serious do you consider this problem? Has it affected the majority of Catholics, or only fringe groups? To what degree?

2. What are the causes of the present religious unrest? Rate the following in importance: 1) the new liturgy; 2) new ideas in theology; 3) changing previous practices without adequate explanation; 4) disrespect for Church authority; 5) the "generation gap" between old and young.

3. Some say the bishops should take a firmer stand in curbing extremists. Others wish the present permissiveness to continue. Which is the right approach?

4. Joe declares: "The upheaval in the Catholic Church is only a reflection of the upheaval in the whole of human society." Is this true? What's going on in the world?

5. We have always had priests and nuns returning to secular life for various reasons. Why do they get so much attention today? Does this do good or harm?

6. John boils when he reads an anti-Catholic article in a Catholic newspaper. "They shouldn't be allowed to print such stuff!" he exclaims. Don, an editor, explodes at the very mention of censorship. Who is right? Should the Church censor religious writing?

7. Pope John was convinced that in free discussion truth will prevail over error. Others say: "He may be correct; but without a pronouncement from the Church, it may take a hundred years or more before the average person knows which side is right and wrong." What do you think?

8. Does the secular press in this country give a balanced presentation of Catholic news? What about the Catholic press? Line up the various publications with which you are

familiar with regard to their position as being right, left or center in the Church today.

9. Some see the diocesan newspaper as an extension of the teaching authority of the bishop. Others look upon it merely as a news medium and would like to see it free from episcopal control. Which side do you prefer?

10. Explain the place of theological opinion in the development of the Catholic teaching. How can one distinguish between opinion and Church doctrine?

11. In his religion classes, Father Z teaches some rather far-out new opinions as though they were official Catholic doctrine. What can and should parents do about this?

CHAPTER II

WHAT HAPPENED AT VATICAN II?

The Church in North America—laity, priests, nuns and even bishops—was almost completely unprepared for the way things turned out at Vatican Council II. This was the result of a number of factors.

1) Americans had remained relatively untouched by World War II. They experienced little of the ferment and unrest, the need to reassert the value of the individual person, which in Europe flowed from the struggle against Nazism and Fascism.

2) Americans, including theologians and bishops, had little or no acquaintance with the new personalist and existential philosophy. This had been developed in Europe, chiefly outside the Church. Introduced by certain European theologians, this philosophy exerted a powerful influence on the deliberations of Vatican II and on Catholic life and teaching since the Council.

3) American Catholics were for the most part unaware of the writings of Protestant theologians, both orthodox and liberal. The ecumenical temper of the times brought these ideas to the attention of Catholic theologians, particularly in Germany, France and Holland.

A good deal of Protestant scholarship was accepted by these theologians and incorporated into their own writings. It will, indeed, be quite a surprise for most Catholics to read such books as *Creative Minds in Contemporary Theology,* and to discover how many of the ideas and how much of the language of some Catholic theologians and writers today has been borrowed in whole or in part from Protestant sources.

This is not to say that all such ideas are wrong, or that they should be rejected. Skillful theologians will take any new values in Protestant scholarship and weave them into the pattern of Catholic thought. Unfortunately, some are not quite so skillful.

Because of the American lack of preparation for the new ideas and the new freedom introduced by the Council, the swing to extremes has perhaps been more pronounced here than in other areas, which were better prepared to understand the new ideas and to put them in proper perspective.

To get a clearer picture, let's go back and look at things as they were when the Council began, October 11, 1962.

GEOGRAPHICAL DISTRIBUTION

The bishops assembled in the huge nave of St. Peter's represented every section of the known world: Europe (39 per cent), Asia (12 per cent), Africa (12 per cent), North America (14 per cent), South America (18 per cent), Central America (3 per cent), and Oceania (2 per cent).

The task placed before this imposing assembly of over 2,300 bishops was the spiritual renewal of the Church in all its aspects so that it might more effectively proclaim the Gospel to modern man, promote peace and unity in the human family, and work for the religious, social and temporal betterment of mankind.

DIFFERENT OPINIONS

At the very start of the Council, it became clear that there were some very different ideas among the cardinals and bishops as to the nature and extent of the spiritual renewal of the Church.

From a practical point of view, the work of the Council consisted in the issuing of sixteen documents. These presented the mind of the Church on the more important problems of the day. However, before these documents reached their final form, they had to undergo a tremendous amount of preparation, debate, correction and even complete revision.

PREPARATION

In order to speed up the work of the Council, the Pope had set up beforehand in Rome a number of preliminary commissions. Their chief task was to draft the documents on various subjects which would be used as a basis for discussion by the Council.

The amount of work involved was simply enormous! The commissions labored intensely for a period of almost three and one-half years, from 1959 to 1962. All the congregations of the Roman Curia were asked to make a comprehensive study and present specific proposals concerning the matters under their authority. Some 2,593 bishops were invited to submit their ideas. The rectors of Catholic universities and the deans of theological faculties around the world were requested to prepare a series of studies on topics which they considered timely and important. All the replies had to be read and catalogued. The material collected in the first year filled sixteen large volumes of almost 10,000 pages.

This was only the beginning! All this material had to be digested, classified and worked into schemas. This required two years of effort by twelve commissions, with a total of 871 members.

Finally, all this material was reduced to twenty schemas which, supposedly, were to be presented to the Council for discussion.

Three months before the start of the Council, Pope John XXIII ordered the first seven schemas to be sent to the members of the Council throughout the world.

Everything so far seemed quiet and peaceful; but a storm was gathering.

RUMBLINGS OF OPPOSITION

The preparatory work for the Council involved the efforts of 871 experts—cardinals, bishops, priests and laymen—representing more than 57 nations. However, anyone who expected that the Council would merely give a rubber stamp approval to the schemas prepared by the commissions was very much mistaken. For behind the scene forces of opposition were gathering which would eventually gain control of the Council and sweep most of the prepared schemas into the wastebasket.

The first organized evidence of this opposition appeared in Holland. Seventeen Dutch bishops and their theologians gathered to discuss the material received from Rome. This group came to the conclusion that the first four documents, which treated mostly of theological matters, were too conservative and traditional. They felt that they did not reflect the advances of recent scholarship and meet the needs of modern man. The document on the liturgy, however, was found acceptable.

THE PLAN

This group determined upon a plan which later proved to be extraordinarily successful, and which actually changed the whole tenor of the Council. The steps involved in this plan were two: 1) to prepare a criticism of the first four documents for circulation among the bishops when they arrived for the Council; 2) to try to get the document on the liturgy placed first on the order of discussion. The purpose of this was to gain time for the circulation of their criticisms of the first four documents.

Each of these steps was accomplished successfully. A severely critical commentary on the first four documents was prepared by the Dominican theologian,

Edward Schillebeeckx, O.P. This commentary was published anonymously in French, English and Latin. It was distributed to the bishops when they arrived in Rome. The second step of the plan, the proposal to treat first the schema on the liturgy, met no opposition and was given immediate approval at the start of the Council.

PICKING THE COMMISSIONS

There was another crucial step in determining the direction in which the Council would proceed. This was the voting to elect the members of the ten Council commissions. These commissions performed a function somewhat similar to that of the committees of the U. S. Congress. They supervised the presentation to the Council of material in their respective fields, for instance, theology, liturgy, religious life, the missions, etc. Each of these commissions was to consist of twenty-five members, of which sixteen were elected and nine appointed by the Pope.

Again the lines of opposition began to form. Before the Council, the German bishops were much disturbed by a report that the Roman Curia had prepared a list of candidates for election. To counteract this, they came up with an alternative proposal. They suggested that the Bishops' Conferences of each of the various nations be permitted to nominate candidates for the commissions. The Germans presented their idea to the French bishops and they agreed to join forces in pushing this plan.

At the first general meeting of the Council, each bishop was handed a booklet containing the names of all the bishops, together with a list of those who had served on the various preparatory commissions. This was the so-called "Curial List," to which the liberal Europeans were opposed. Early in this first session,

Cardinal Liénart, of France, requested the floor. He made the suggestion that the elections to the commissions be postponed for a few days so that the bishops could study the qualifications of the candidates. Such a request, seconded by Cardinal Frings, head of the German Conference of Bishops, could scarcely be denied. Hence the Council sessions were adjourned for three days.

The Germans and French recognized that by themselves they could not swing enough votes to assure election of their candidates to the commissions. So they proposed to the bishops of Austria, Holland, Switzerland and Belgium that they present a combined list of candidates. To this were added the names of forty-three liberal-minded candidates of other countries and sixteen bishops from Africa. In this way the list of the North European group was given an international flavor, and numerous votes from outside Europe could be expected at the very start.

Again careful planning paid off. Of the 109 candidates proposed by this group, 79 were elected to the various commissions. This total constituted 49 per cent of all the elected members. Other national conferences of bishops submitted lists of candidates; but these lacked unity and organization. It soon became clear that the combination headed by the North Europeans was strong enough to take over the leadership which the Roman Curia had expected to assume.

DIVISIONS OF OPINION

To describe the differences of opinions between the bishops at the Council as being merely liberal vs. conservative, or diocesan vs. curial would be to oversimplify. First of all, the difference between liberal and conservative is purely relative. It depends on one's point of view. To a person who holds opinions on the extreme right, everyone else is too liberal. To the person on the extreme left, everyone else is too conservative.

Among the bishops at the Council, a few were hardcore conservatives and a few far-out liberals. However, the vast majority fell into neither category. They ranged through every degree of opinion. As a result, after matters were hammered out in debate, the final stand was usually pretty much in the middle. That's why the actual documents issued by the Council contain nothing that can be classified as radical.

DUMPING THE CURIAL PREPARATIONS

We return to the commentary written by Father Schillebeeckx for the Dutch bishops, and circulated anonymously at the beginning of the Council. It suggested that all the first five documents presented by the preparatory commission, except the one on the liturgy, be completely rewritten. This became the goal of the German-French bishops and their allies. This group was organized and well-prepared. Its members not only knew what they wanted, but they had skillfully prepared criticisms of the curial documents for use in debate, and possessed alternative schemas to present to the Council. Consequently, they succeeded in having most of the previously prepared documents sent to the various Council commissions for revision. Since they had also succeeded in getting control of these commissions, it was not hard to predict that the new schemas would reflect their ideas and their spirit.

This does not mean that the Council suddenly swung around to an extreme liberal point of view. No, but what it did do was to accept and emphasize certain ideas which had previously, at least to some extent, been minimized or neglected.

Such ideas are, for instance: 1) the personal dignity, rights and freedom of the individual human being; 2) participation of all the faithful in the liturgy; 3) the spirit of ecumenism; 4) the vocation of the laity to share in the apostolic mission of the Church; 5) the collegial union of all bishops with the pope in the government of the whole Church; 6) more democratic procedures in the exercise of authority; 7) an encouragement to dialogue on all levels—between bishops themselves, between bishops and priests, between clergy and laity; 8) more extensive use of the Bible in the catechetical and preaching work of imparting the word of God; 9) greater emphasis on the Church as a mystery, a divine intervention in the world, as the people of God, on its pilgrim way through the desert of life to the kingdom of heaven; 10) recognition of the duty of all Christians to work to build a better world here on earth.

As the Council progressed, the documents presenting these ideas were hammered out in their final form only after long and serious debate by bishops of every cast of mind. One who reads the actual documents promulgated by the Council will be struck by their moderation. They reflect the spirit of progress and renewal, but retain the ancient truths and values.

However, since the Council, not all theologians and writers have observed the same prudence and moderation. Not only have some accepted the positive, personal and existential values mentioned above, but they have also uncritically adopted and proclaimed some of the erroneous ideas with which these values have been associated by writers outside the Church.

How this all came about, we will try to explain in succeeding chapters. Our thesis is that the confusion and anguish of many in the Church today results from the introduction into Catholic philosophy and theology of certain principles which are incompatible with the Catholic faith. These false principles have been introduced because of the mistaken belief that they are a necessary part of the positive and progressive ideas proclaimed by Vatican Council II. Actually, we must separate such ideas from the false subjective and relative philosophy with which they have become entwined.

Discussion Points

1. Review the condition of the Church in America at the beginning of Vatican II with relation to the following points: 1) growth and vitality; 2) position and influence; 3) relationship between clergy and laity; 4) Catholic education; 5) vocations to the priesthood and religious life; 6) relationship between Catholics and other religious bodies; 7) the Church's understanding of her mission.

2. What changes have taken place in each of these areas since Vatican II? Do you think things have gotten better or worse? To what extent? What reasons would you assign for the change?

3. Were American Catholics prepared for the impact of Vatican II? If not, why not?

4. The Council has been portrayed in American publications mostly as a contest between modern progressives and die-hard conservatives. Do you think this gave a fair picture of the persons and issues involved? Why?

5. What has been the influence of European theologians upon American Catholics since Vatican II? Some have expressed a wish that such theologians would go home and let us work out our own problems. What would you say about this?

6. A number of European theologians have been amazed at the speed with which many Americans have shifted from one religious extreme to the other. What reason would you assign for this? The American character? The temper of the times? A lack of understanding of the deeper issues?

7. Relate how the northern European bishops arrived at a position of leadership at Vatican II.

8. Which do you consider the most important ideas developed in Vatican II? Why the emphasis on the rights and dignity of the individual person? Show how this emphasis affects the new approach to ecumenism, the sharing of the laity in the apostolate, the encouragement to dialogue on all levels, freedom of conscience, working for a better world on earth, etc.

9. The text states that some writers have associated true personalist values with a false subjectivist philosophy which is incompatible with the Catholic faith. Can you explain what this means?

CHAPTER III

THE NEW AND THE OLD THEOLOGY

In order to understand the differences of opinion among the bishops at the Vatican Council and among theologians today, we must make some very important distinctions. Not all parts of what go by the general name of "Catholic teaching" have an equal weight of divine authority behind them.

At the very heart of the Church's teaching is the divine revelation by which God reveals himself to men and makes known the hidden purpose of His will to save all men and unite them to himself through Christ, His incarnate Son. The story of this revelation, or what is called "salvation history," was first made known to us through the patriarchs and prophets of Israel, as we read in the Old Testament. All this, however, was only a preparation for the complete revelation of himself which God made through Jesus Christ, the Word made flesh.

In His goodness, God willed that the message of salvation brought by Christ should be handed on to all the generations of mankind until the end of time. Therefore, Christ established His Church upon the foundation stones of St. Peter and the apostles and gave it the commission to preach the Gospel to all men. It is by this apostolic preaching that the world is to be saved. The gospels are the summary and written record of this preaching of the apostles.

REVELATION AND FAITH

On the part of those who hear it, the response, made by men of good will, moved by God's grace, is *faith*. This is not merely an assent of the mind. It is a total acceptance and commitment of the believer to God through Jesus Christ.

However, it is important to note that faith, as described in the New Testament, is not only faith in Christ. It is also faith in the apostolic preaching, in what St. Paul calls "the word of faith" (Rom. 10:8).

The Catholic faith is based on an objective revelation, made by God through Jesus Christ, and presented to men in every age through the teaching of the Church.

That is why Christianity is incompatible with any philosophy which holds that man cannot know objective truth. Nor can it be reconciled with the position that the essential content of faith changes from age to age. In other words, the Catholic faith cannot be squared with a philosophy of *idealism, subjectivism* or *relativism*.

We will explain these ideas as we go along. It is enough now to know that idealism declares that man cannot know things as they are in themselves, but only as they are in his mind. From this it would follow that he cannot know objective truth. All his knowledge, even of religion, would be purely subjective. Since, according to this opinion, man cannot know objective truth, for him all expressions of truth, including religion, will be purely relative. That is, they will change from age to age in response to man's different viewpoints and needs.

This philosophy of idealism, with its consequences of subjectivism and relativism, has been setting the Protestant churches in turmoil for more than a century. Since Vatican II, it has begun to appear, consciously or unconsciously, in the writings of a number of Catholic authors. Usually it is put forward under the guise of "presenting the old truths in new language," or "speaking to the contemporary mind." Both these objectives are laudable. However, we must make sure that the old truths, the essential content of God's revelation, are still present in the new language, and that the essential content has not been changed.

The word of God, the objective revelation made by God through Christ and proclaimed in the teaching of the Church, cannot change from age to age. Of course, man's understanding of this word can deepen, and the language in which it is expressed can take different forms. But the essential content must remain the same, and the new language must truly express this content.

WHAT IS THEOLOGY?

Over and above the revelation given to the Church by Christ and the apostles, Catholic teaching includes what we call *theology*. This results from the application of the human mind to revealed truths in order to deduce further conclusions and to make practical applications.

However, since theology makes use of the fallible human mind in deducing its conclusions and making its applications, there is room for differences of opinion. The deeper and more complex the question, the greater room there is for such differences of opinion.

From what has been said, it is clear that theology is an organized body of knowledge, at which we arrive by applying human reason to divinely revealed truth. But the trouble is that men do not always reason the same. In fact, they often arrive at very different conclusions about things because of their different backgrounds, education, interests and general philosophy of life. This holds true when they reason about religious matters, even though they accept the same basic Christian truths.

THEOLOGY TODAY

That is what is happening in the Church today. We have the conflict of two different philosophies, or ways of looking at things, which have been battling each other since men first began to think about themselves and the world around them. The first of these philosophies, or mental approaches, begins with *the world outside of man*. It holds that man can know the external world, of which he is a part. This world is made up of real things, with definite and determined natures and modes of operation. Man comes in contact with this world by the use of his senses. He can study this world and observe its laws. Under the changing phenomena known by his senses, he can reason to that which is permanent and unchanging, to the essences of things. From the way things act, he can deduce their intrinsic nature.

The second philosophy begins not with the external world, but *inside the mind of man*. This is concerned with the way things seem to man, with his sensations, thoughts, feelings and emotions. It deals with the concrete and personal character of human existence, with its changing states of consciousness, its longings and anxieties, and its constant need for decisions.

You might say at this point: "I don't see that these two philosophies, or approaches to things, are really contradictory, or necessarily opposed to each other. There is a real external world, whose nature man can discover by making use of his faculties of knowledge. There is also the world of human consciousness, of which man becomes aware by reflecting on his own acts—his sensations, thoughts, feelings and decisions. What man must do is blend these two worlds together into a coherent whole."

NO CONTRADICTION

You are right! There is no necessary contradiction between an objective and a personalist philosophy. Each can, and must recognize the truths and values asserted by the other. They are not opposed, but complementary ways of looking at total reality.

This is true and most important. Actually, it is the way in which the common sense of mankind thinks of the relation between man and the world around him.

Unfortunately, however, as we will explain more in detail later on, certain philosophers have driven a wedge between the mind of man and the external world. They assert that man cannot make any certain judgments about the world outside his mind. How does he know there is any real world at all? Perhaps it is all a delusion. And even if there is an external world, how can he be sure that his own process of knowing is not distorting the picture of it? Because such a philosophy imprisons man in his own mind, and makes the object of his knowledge his own ideas and not the real world, it is called *idealism*.

This philosophy of idealism has profoundly affected modern thought. It has distorted the personalist approach to philosophy which is natural to the human mind. Moreover, since it denies man's ability to know objective truth, it is incompatible with Christianity. For this is based on the acceptance of an objective revelation made by God to man through Christ and proclaimed in the teaching of the Church.

Because it centers attention upon the interior world of human thought and feeling, idealistic philosophy has made us more keenly aware of certain personal and existential values which had been, at least to some extent, minimized or forgotten. This is its great contribution to modern thought. However, the real values in the personalist and existential approach must be separated from the false subjectivism and relativism with which these values have been surrounded by the idealistic philosophy in which they were developed.

This is the task of Catholic theology today, and it is going to take some time before it is completed. In the meantime, we have a great deal of confusion and considerable anguish. More than a few theologians, popular writers and journalists have felt that in order to assert the new personal and existential values, it is necessary to reject the old essential values. Furthermore, some have failed to separate true personalist and existential values from the subjectivism and relativism with which they have been presented by writers outside the Church.

POLAR POSITIONS IN THE CHURCH

The word "polarization" has become so popular today that no self-respecting author can write a book without including it. It is a scientific word referring to the fact that iron filings will gather in striking patterns at positive and negative poles in response to an electric current.

Before we get started on a discussion of the particular issues in the Church today, it may be useful to present a bird's-eye view of the ideas around which such polarizations have occurred in the Church since Vatican II.

Those who have some acquaintance with philosophy and theology will immediately grasp the pattern which emerges. We ask the others to be patient. There are some big words and difficult ideas in this list. As we move along in this book, we will try to explain their meaning and the relationship between them.

THE "NEW" THEOLOGY

The so-called "new" theology is, first of all, *personal.* That is, it approaches Christian revelation from the viewpoint of man. It is not interested in presenting a systematic elaboration of religious truth, but in bringing home what religion means for man. Hence it bypasses, or gives scant treatment to such questions as the nature of God as He is in himself, or to God as Creator and Governor of the universe. It centers attention on what meaning God has for man.

The new theology is *existential*. It looks at religion from the viewpoint of what it means to man in his day by day existence. How will it help man meet the problems, overcome the obstacles and make the right decisions in his daily life?

It is *dynamic*, concerned with action rather than with thought. It emphasizes concern for everything human, involvement in man's struggle for a better life, each man's duty to work for a better world here on earth. "Don't just stand there; pitch in and help," is its slogan.

It emphasizes the *subjective*. Faith is presented as a personal response, an act in which man encounters God, in which he establishes an I-Thou relationship with God.

The Church is presented as the *mystery* of God's saving love, as the people of God on the march toward the eternal kingdom.

The new theology stresses the *freedom* of each man as a unique and responsible individual, called to develop his own personality under the influence of grace. It tends, therefore, to emphasize the rights of the individual conscience, and to restrict the place of law and the exercise of authority.

Over and over, we are reminded of the supreme importance of *love*—the love of God and of our fellow men. The liturgy, especially the Eucharist, is at once the symbol and cause of this love between Christians. Nor is this love to be confined only to those who are members of the faith. It should flow out in an ecumenical spirit, and try to bring all mankind into the unity of faith and love.

TRADITIONAL THEOLOGY

Traditional theology is God-centered. It begins, under the light of revelation, to study the nature of God as He is in himself. It goes on to consider God as Creator and Governor of the universe and, particularly, of man, whom He has called to share His own divine life. God's will for man is revealed in the objective revelation which He made in the Old and New Testament and which was confided by Jesus Christ to His Church. This Church is a visible body with an organized structure. To her, Christ gave power to teach the Gospel to all men. He also gave her power to govern men on the way of salvation, and to sanctify them through the sacraments.

The mission of the Church is to all mankind. Therefore all men have the obligation of hearing and accepting the truth when it is presented to them. Faith is, then, a response of the mind and will, moved by God's grace, accepting the revelation which God has made of himself to mankind.

This faith, however, must not remain sterile. It must flow out in acts of love of God and of one's fellow men. Living this life of faith, hope and love, with which he is endowed at Baptism, each man grows ever more like to Christ. When life is done, the light of faith will blossom into the light of glory and, possessing God by knowledge and love in the beatific vision, man will share God's happiness with all the members of Christ's Mystical Body throughout eternity.

This summary of the new and old approach to theology is by no means complete. However, it does bring out a good many of the areas in which there are differences of approach. *The important thing to notice is that all the ideas presented on each side are positive values!* They do not contradict, but complement each other. Each presents a partial view of truth and must be blended with the correlative value on the other side to attain the total truth.

Throughout our discussions, we will balance the new

ideas against the old, trying to discover what is good and true and useful in each.

As we proceed, we will find that, in general, each side is usually correct in the values it asserts, mistaken insofar as it ignores or denies the values of the other side.

We must try earnestly to keep our minds open to truth wherever it may lie, and to overcome personal prejudices that may blind us to the total truth.

Our discussions should be carried out with sincerity, with prudence, and above all with charity. No light is ever brought on any matter by introducing emotion or by quarreling. And always, we should take as guide the teaching authority of the Church, which has been given to us precisely so that all men may come to the knowledge of God and find the path of salvation easily, with solid certainty and with no trace of error.

At present, there is plenty of room for difference of opinion. We cannot pretend to say the final word, nor to discover all the answers. This may take a theologian as great as was St. Thomas in his day. However, we can't just stand around and wait for him. We must get started on the task and help, in what measure we can, to break the way.

Discussion Points

1. What is divine revelation? Is this a natural or a supernatural concept?

2. What is meant by "salvation history"? Show the relationship between the Old Testament and the New.

3. Explain the difference between the Catholic and Protestant interpretation of the role of the Church and the Bible in the transmission of divine revelation.

4. Is there any promise that God will reveal the meaning of various parts of the Bible to each individual? Can

the Holy Spirit inspire contradictory interpretations of the word of God? How, then, can we have so many different religious sects?

5. What is meant by theology? Explain the function of human reason in the construction of various systems of theology. How is it possible for men who hold the same basic truths of faith to have different theological opinions?

6. Throughout this book we will often use the terms *idealism, subjectivism* and *relativism*. Refer to the text and get the exact meaning of these terms.

7. Describe the philosophy of idealism. How does it drive a wedge between the mind of man and the external world?

8. Why would an idealist normally be more conscious of personal than of objective values?

9. Is it better for a human being to be clear-headed, impersonal, cool and logical, or to be warm, personal, emotional and dedicated? Analyze the strengths and weaknesses of each personality. Which qualities should a person try to develop?

10. Describe the "new" theology. What is meant by saying that it is personal, existential and dynamic? Describe its emphasis on the sense of community and on the importance of love.

11. Contrast the "new" theology with the "old." Bring out clearly the point that each approach presents positive values which must be integrated into a complete theology.

12. Tom asserts: "In order to get in line with Vatican II, we must reject all the old theological ideas and present a purely personalist, man-centered theology." Mary objects: "In order to safeguard the Catholic faith, we must reject the personalist approach to theology and emphasize that true religion is God-centered, not man-centered." Which is right?

CHAPTER IV

HOW DID IT ALL GET STARTED?

On the walls of more than one hundred caves in southern Europe, there can be found magnificent paintings of ice age animals, portrayed with astonishing skill by the hands of prehistoric men about ten thousand years before Christ. One remarkable feature about them is that the animals are pictured with splendid realism. You can see massive muscles bunched in tension, heads raised in alertness to danger, horns lowered for the thrust at the enemy. On the contrary, wherever human beings appear, they are usually in caricature, represented by just a few simple lines, something like the drawing of a child in kindergarten.

MAN vs. WORLD

There has been a lot of speculation about the reason for this; but it brings out an important fact. Primitive men were more concerned with investigating the world around them, than with studying themselves. To them the world was very real. It was not dependent upon them; but they were very dependent upon it. By no effort of theirs did the red ball of the sun rise in the morning and darkness close upon them at night. The storms broke, the rain fell, and the rivers ran without their consent. They hunted animals for their food. If they were successful, they feasted; if not, they starved.

They were a part of the world in which they lived, and realized they must accommodate themselves to its laws. Never for an instant did it occur to them that all these things—the sun and the moon, the birds and trees and animals, the rivers and lakes — might be merely a product of their own minds.

This same objective view of the relationship between man and the world in which he lives prevailed among the ancient Jews. It has been superbly expressed in the final chapters of the book of Job, certainly one of the literary masterpieces of all time.

Where were you when I laid the earth's foundations?
    Tell me, since you are so well-informed! . . .
Who pent up the sea behind closed doors
    when it leapt tumultuous out of the womb,
when I wrapped it in a robe of mist
    and made black clouds its swaddling bands;
when I marked the bounds it was not to cross
    and made it fast with a bolted gate? . . .
Have you ever in your life given orders to the
        morning
    or sent the dawn to its post? . . .
Does the hawk take flight on your advice
    when he spreads his wings to travel south?
Does the eagle soar at your command
    to make her eyrie in the heights? (Job 38:4-39:28)

The great artists of the Renaissance had this same objective view of the reality of the world in which they lived. Hence they considered imitation of this reality to be a valid function of the artist. Indeed, in biographies of such men as Michelangelo, we read how carefully they studied the nature of things in order to portray them with utmost fidelity.

SUBJECTIVISM IN ART

Go to a gallery of modernistic art and you will see a tremendous change. No longer will you find in many pictures objects that can be identified as existing in the real world. Instead, you will see splashes and patterns of color that may, or may not, convey any meaning to you. A picture may be entitled "Girl on a Swing," but there is nothing that any ordinary man can identify either as a girl or as a swing. Indeed, more than once it has facetiously been said that if you turned a chimpanzee loose with a brush and a bucket of paint, he could produce the same type of picture.

What's this all about? Have modern artists suddenly "gone off their rocker?" No, it is simply that *relativism* is dominant in modern art. Many artists reject the concept of objective truth and hold that all reality is subjective. This means that each individual must construct his own reality, however arbitrary and even absurd this may seem. In the past, men agreed that a general and basic reality existed, which was waiting for artistic revelation. Now this security is removed, and the artist is trying to sell his own personal concept of reality, especially his own feelings and emotions. If you can share this emotion with him while looking at his picture, he is pleased; but if you can't, he is not overly disturbed.

LITERATURE AND ENTERTAINMENT

The same holds true to a great extent in the fields of literature and entertainment. Back in the old days, if you picked up a book or read a story in a magazine, you could pretty well depend that it would have a good, substantial plot, that the characters would be like those you meet in real life, and that the action would progress in orderly stages. The same held true for movies and plays.

Now, however, you may pick up a best seller or read a magazine story, and find that it has no plot at all. It merely snips a few moments from the life of an individual. For instance, it may describe the thoughts and feelings of a young teacher the first time he walks into his classroom. Or it may merely follow the stream of consciousness of the characters without order or design. The author is concerned not with things that happen, but with what goes on inside men's minds and hearts.

As a result of this concentration on the subjective, the inner experience of the individual, you will notice that often modern movies, plays and TV programs, as well as painting, sculpture and other art forms, no longer try to portray real people in real life situations. They search for bizarre and fantastic characters and plots, in which the emphasis is on the subhuman or the superhuman. No doubt, too, this is at least partially the explanation for the increasing use of LSD and other hallucigenic drugs. Those who use them are seeking new mental and emotional experiences, and are not concerned that these are causing them to drift farther and farther away from reality.

SUBJECTIVISM IN RELIGION

This same emphasis on the subjective — on the thoughts and feelings of men—with a consequent de-emphasis or denial of the objective has also manifested itself in the field of religion. This has been the cause of great upheaval in some Protestant circles for over a century. It is manifested in such statements as the declaration of Bishop Pike that Christians should discard the doctrine of the Trinity. He is not at all concerned with whether there is, or is not, a trinity of persons in God. The objective truth or falsity of the doctrine doesn't interest him. He merely asserts that this doctrine has no meaning or value for modern man; therefore, he says, let's get rid of it.

The same holds true for the "God is dead" movement. These people have not made a thorough study and come to the conclusion that there is no God. Rather, they say that, in view of modern man's mastery over the sciences, he has no need of God. Therefore, they declare, let's get rid of Him, and build a world in which religion has no part.

This emphasis on the subjective elements of religion, this man-centered and highly personal approach to religious matters, has today gained an entrance into the Catholic Church.

Don't get excited by this statement, as though sizable portions of the Church were falling into heresy. As we mentioned before, we have to learn to see both sides of things. The subjective approach is not of itself wrong. There is an inner world of human experience, of thought and feeling, and it is very important to man. It becomes false and mistaken, in religion as in other areas, only when it disregards or denies the existence of objective truth and reality.

How did this apparent conflict between subjective and objective, between thought and reality, between relative and absolute truth get started?

DESCARTES

The beginnings of subjectivism as an approach to philosophy can be traced back to the French philosopher, mathematician and scientist, René Descartes (1596-1650). As a young man, Descartes conceived the very ambitious plan of rebuilding the whole structure of human knowledge after the pattern of mathematics. In order to do this, he would have to tear down the old structures that had been set up by others before him. As a tool, he used what he called "the methodic doubt." He would doubt every statement, every opinion, every item of knowledge, until he came to some foundation where doubt was impossible.

He rejects the evidence of the senses. "For," he asserts, "they are deceptive, and it is prudent never to trust absolutely what has once deceived us." We may even, he says, "doubt whether there be any earth or sky or any other body." "For, supposing that nothing of the sort exists, I can still have the impression of their existence. This is evident from the way things appear in madness and in dreams."

Nor can we be sure of what appear to be the simplest and clearest truths. "How do I know that God has not so arranged it that I am deceived each time I add two and three together, or number the sides of a square, or form some judgments still more simple, if indeed anything more simple can be imagined?"

After all other knowledge is thus disposed of, only one thing remains: *the fact of my own thought.* This I am sure of; this I can never doubt. But in order to think, I must exist. *Cogito, ergo sum—I think, therefore I am*—behold the bedrock of all human knowledge!

Upon this foundation, Descartes built an elaborate structure of philosophy; but it was all the product of his own mind, not built by gathering and weighing external evidence.

I think, therefore I am, does not appear at first sight to be too radical a statement. Nevertheless, by that sentence Descartes dug the pit into which practically all modern philosophy has fallen. Why? *Because he made his own thought the primary object of his act of knowing!* He locked himself inside his own mind and destroyed any possibility of building a bridge to the world of reality. For how can I ever be sure that my mind is not distorting the picture of reality? How, indeed, can I be sure that anything really exists outside my mind? It may all be a dream, a delusion. Consequently, he said, a man can never really be certain of anything outside his own mind.

Descartes was a religious man. He believed in God and accepted the truths of Christianity. He acknowledged the existence of a real world outside his mind; but he did so only by making an act of faith in God.

God, he said, would not allow man to have a clear and distinct idea that something is true, without himself guaranteeing its objective truth. Needless to say, it did not take long for those who followed Descartes to reject this conviction. The most important of these is the German philosopher, Immanuel Kant (1724-1804).

KANT

Like Descartes, Kant set for himself the formidable task of reviewing all knowledge in order to answer the questions: What can I know? What ought I do? What may I hope for?

The first of these questions, the nature and validity of human knowledge, he investigates in his book *The Critique of Pure Reason.* Though he proceeds in an entirely different manner, he arrives at the same conclusion as Descartes: that man can never have direct and certain knowledge of anything outside his own mind.

We cannot, he says, know reality, things as they are in themselves, but only the appearances of things, because our faculties impose their own forms upon that which enters the mind. Neither sensation, judgment nor reasoning can give us a valid picture of the world outside ourselves. We can never reach the *noumenon,* the thing as it is in itself, but only the *phenomenon,* the thing as it appears to us. Neither science nor philosophy can enable us to reach the substance, or essence of things. Nor can they tell us what the soul is, what matter is, or what God is.

Like Descartes, Kant had attempted to tear down the whole structure of previously existing human knowledge, only to build it up again on what he considered a more solid foundation. For him this foundation was the *imperative command of conscience* which every man experiences in himself. You will note that again for Kant, as for Descartes, the ultimate test of truth is not found in external reality, but is something in man's own mind. This command of conscience, he declares, imposes itself with insistence and with certainty. Once the voice of conscience tells me that "I ought" to do something, I cannot escape from the certainty that I am obliged to do what my conscience commands. However, I can choose to obey or to disobey.

It is clear from what has been said that for Kant religion is reduced to a system of moral conduct. He wants to get rid of all dogmatic definitions, and bring about the kingdom of God on earth by establishing a reign of duty. For him, even ancient Christian dogmas, such as the Trinity, should be taught as symbols of moral values.

IMPACT OF KANT

The influence of Kant on philosophy and religion has been enormous, and it has continued until today. Even more than Descartes who started the trend, he can be called the father of modern idealism. Almost every philosophical position in the western world, except the realism of Aristotle and St. Thomas, can be traced back in some measure to his influence.

RELATIVE TRUTH

The philosophers who have followed Kant accept his doctrine that the mind of man cannot of itself attain objective truth, that is, truth about things as they are outside the mind. However, most of them reject the whole structure he built up with relation to conscience and the moral law. The trouble is that this leaves them without any standard whatsoever by which to measure truth. Consequently, for them there is no certain and absolute truth. Everything is relative, a matter of opinion. In this bog of the relativity of truth, certain types of philosophy and theology have floundered for more than one hundred and fifty years, with profound effect upon the social, religious and intellectual life of mankind.

Of course, the development of Kant's thought in the more than a century and a half since his death, has not followed a single line. In fact, it has split into some remarkably divergent positions. Modern agnosticism and atheism, evolutionary pantheism, secularism and Communism all spring to some extent from the influence of Kant. So likewise, do many of the positions adopted by liberal Protestants and by existentialist philosophers.

In succeeding chapters, we will attempt to trace the origin and development of these ideas, and their influence upon Catholic thought today.

Discussion Points

1. Can a man seriously doubt the existence of a real world outside his mind? What would happen if he tried to live according to such a doubt?

2. Discuss the passage from Job in the text and show how it brings out belief in a real world created by God, in which things act in accordance with the laws of nature.

3. An artist, it is said, once painted a rose which appeared so real that a bee tried to sip its nectar. Would this be the goal of most modern artists? What are the latter trying to convey with their various patterns of color?

4. Point out other manifestations of subjectivism and relativism in modern life. Have you read any books or seen any movies produced from this point of view?

5. Steve says: "This excessive preoccupation with man's inner thoughts and emotions is producing a sick generation. Instead of getting out and working and enjoying nor-

mal healthy pleasures, too many young people are lying around smoking pot or taking drugs in order to escape from reality to a world of dreams." To what extent is this statement true?

6.   Father Dan, chaplain at a secular university, comments: "The reason for this retreat from reality is that modern secular education has taken away everything that gives life a real meaning. Young people are left with nothing to believe in, nothing to hope for, nothing to live or die for. That's why they want to escape from the world and turn in on themselves." Is there any truth in this?

7.   Explain the importance of Descartes in the history of philosophy? Review his attempt to rebuild the whole structure of human knowledge. Show how his principle "I think therefore I am," contains in itself the germ of idealistic philosophy. How did Descartes attempt to bridge the gap he had placed between reality and the mind of man?

8.   What reason did Kant give for declaring that man cannot know reality, but only the appearances of things?

9.   Describe Kant's attempt to rebuild the whole structure of human knowledge in terms of moral values.

10.   Point out some of the consequences of Kant's philosophy in the fields of philosophy and religion.

11.   To what extent have Kant's ideas influenced modern thought?

CHAPTER V

WHAT IS EXISTENTIALISM?

In order to understand what has been going on in the Church since Vatican II, it is necessary to have some understanding of the philosophy of *existentialism,* or *personalism.*

Immediately, many will ask: "What is existentialism?"

The answer to that is not easy. For existentialism is not a definite, set body of philosophical or theological doctrines. In fact, it rejects any attempt to organize ideas or beliefs into a system.

Neither is existentialism identified with any religious denomination. Some of the most famous existentialists, like Jean Paul Sartre and Albert Camus, are atheists. Heidegger, sometimes called the father of existentialism, is an agnostic. Others are Catholic, for instance, Marcel and Wust. Karl Barth, Rudolf Bultmann and Reinhold Niebuhr are Protestants. Still others, like Jaspers, although religious, belong to no particular denomination.

Nor should existentialism be equated with "beatniks" or "hippies," although both these movements reflect a distorted version of the existential concern about the freedom of the individual.

Well, you may ask, if it is not a science, not a philosophy, not a religion, not a mass movement, what precisely is existentialism? We can describe it in this way: *Existentialism is a mental approach, a way of thinking, which studies every problem from the viewpoint of the consciousness of the individual human person.*

In this approach, man is the center, and everything is considered with relation to his thoughts, his feelings, his personal problems, his fears, anxieties and longings.

A few examples will help to bring this idea home:

1) To the question: "Why did God make me?" the old answer was: "God made me to know Him, to love Him and to serve Him, etc." The existentialist would answer: "God made me because He loves me."

2) To the question: "What is a mother?" the essential answer would be: "A mother is a woman who has borne one or more children." The existentialist would answer: "A mother is one who loves and cares for me."

IMPORTANCE OF THE INDIVIDUAL

Soren Kierkegaard, a Danish theologian who is considered one of the forerunners of existentialism, once said that he would like his epitaph to be: "Here lies *That Individual.*"

This is the spirit that pervades all existential thought. It rebels against anything which depersonalizes the individual. This explains its bias against totalitarianism, against authority, against centralization in any shape or form. The person, the individual is paramount.

EVERYWHERE TODAY

The existential approach has not only made its influence felt in philosophy and theology, but it has crept into every nook and cranny of modern society. You'll find it in modern psychology, with its emphasis on the search for "man's true self." Art and literature are saturated with existential themes that treat of man's alienation, his frustrated freedom, and his meaningless existence. The same holds true of the theatre, and particularly of the movies, in which the roving eye of the camera can so easily simulate the kaleidoscopic patterns of the changing states of human consciousness.

GERMAN-FRENCH EXPORT

Existentialism has been exported to all parts of the

world from both France and Germany. For it is in these two countries that its principal proponents reside. We find among them men with German names like Karl Jaspers and Martin Heidegger; or French names like Jean Paul Sartre, Albert Camus, and Gabriel Marcel. Soren Kierkegaard was a Dane and Friedrich Nietzsche a German; but these last two are forerunners, rather than existentialists in the true sense.

IMPACT ON THEOLOGY

The existentialist thought of these philosophers has had profound influence on many liberal German theologians, such as Karl Barth, Rudolf Bultmann, Emil Brunner, Paul Tillich and Reinhold Niebuhr.

These philosophers and theologians by their writings, and especially by contacts in the universities, influenced a number of German and French Catholic theologians to accept phases of the existential approach.

Then came Vatican Council II. We have described how the North European group of bishops, headed by Germany and France, exerted a dominant influence in the Council. Moreover, their theologians wrote the revised versions of the more important schemas which served as basis of discussion in the Council. As a result, these schemas reflect a strong tone of personalism.

Of course, as was mentioned before, these documents were debated by bishops of every cast of mind. Some of the schemas were sent back for correction four or five times. The final version blended both the new personalism and the traditional acceptance of objective truth.

To put it another way, the Council accepted many personalist values; but it did not accept subjectivism or relativism. Again and again its documents, particularly the constitutions on revelation and on the Church, bring home the message that God has made an objective revelation of His plan to save mankind through His Son, Jesus Christ. Through the teaching of Christ's Church man can have absolute certitude about what he must believe and do to attain salvation.

BEWILDERED GUIDES

Unfortunately, many of those who have spoken and written on theology since Vatican II have not recognized this distinction between true personalist values and the subjectivism and relativism with which they have been encapsuled by such men as Heidegger, Sartre, Camus and other agnostic or atheistic philosophers and liberal Protestant theologians. This is all the more true of certain amateur theologians, journalists and popular writers and speakers. They think that to be up-to-date, they have to buy the whole package. As a result, they produce in those who read and hear them profound confusion and dismay.

To show the sources of this confusion, let's examine a little more deeply the manner in which existential ideas are presented by men outside the Church.

CONCRETE vs. ABSTRACT

The existentialist begins with the assertion that, due to the influence of the Greeks, the philosophy of the western world has been dominated by the concept of *essence*. It has been searching for the abstract, universal, unchanging aspects of things, instead of looking at the concrete, individual, ever-changing character of human *existence*. Man, they say, does not live his life alone and isolated, amid the dry bones of intellectual and rational principles. He lives rather on the level of the concrete and personal. The basic character of his human existence is that of consciousness, change, movement, feeling, involvement and decision.

One who tries to separate man from his human condition, from the historical reality in which he lives, distorts the true picture. He becomes irrelevant to the realities of human existence. Hence, the existentialist says, let's get rid of all the old abstract ideas of classical philosophy, such as substance, accidents, essence, soul, virtue and the like. These ideas are all abstract. They fail to do justice to the concrete, individual character of human life. There is no such thing as "man." There are only individual men, like Tom Smith and Pete Jones, with their joys and hopes and fears, their struggles and anxieties, their anguish and suffering, and finally their inevitable encounter with death which puts an end to their brief existence.

The true existentialist wants to have nothing to do with abstract thought and cool intellectual detachment. Therefore he tries to get his ideas across by novels, plays, poems and movies, in which he can stir up emotion and awaken concern. The typical existentialist is not a calm, clear-eyed statesman, dispassionately figuring out the rational answers to such problems as civil rights or war in southeast Asia. He is out on a picket line, showing his indignation over "police brutality," or at a protest meeting shouting slogans about peace.

"AUTHENTIC EXISTENCE"

Because of his insistence on the fact that each individual is completely unique, the existentialist is greatly concerned with what he calls "authentic existence." This means that each man must sincerely strive to be himself, to avoid everything artificial or phony. Consequently, he rebels against doing anything merely because it is conventional, or because it is imposed upon him by authority. An extreme manifestation of this is the "hippie," with his matted beard, his dirty clothes, his uninhibited sex life. This is his way of saying to the world: "I'll have none of your artificial standards and values; love is the only thing that counts!"

But the matter goes much deeper than the external. The existentialist emphasizes that every man is free. He can lose or win himself. He loses himself, his freedom, his uniqueness, by conforming to any pattern of morals or belief that is set for him by others. For then he is not being himself. He is surrendering his freedom. He is becoming a puppet in the hands of others. Man can save himself only by being true to himself in the loneliness of his unique human existence, by resolute decisions, often after much struggle and anguish, in the concrete situations he meets in life.

What it means to be a man in the true sense, therefore, is best discovered by exploring such basic human reactions as fear, shame, guilt, anxiety, concern. These are man's reactions to a world in which he finds himself thrown without his consent, to a world which presses in on him from every side, and which will eventually destroy him by death.

"SO SOON TO DIE"

This consciousness of mortality, of the fact that "man, scarcely born, is so soon to die," weighs heavily upon many existentialist writers. A good number, as mentioned, are atheists or agnostics. Even for those who are Christians, the concept of personal immortality is very hard to fit into their system. They reject the idea of the soul as a permanent vital principle in man. For them, the whole of human life is pictured merely as a succession of changing states of consciousness, without permanent substratum, or foundation. With such a philosophy, it is hard to see how anything can remain of man after his consciousness is terminated by death.

In fact, many existential philosophers, such as Heidegger, Sartre and Camus, openly declare that any idea of personal immortality is a delusion. The doctrine of some liberal Protestants, such as Bultmann, Tillich and the "God is dead" crowd, amounts to the same thing, even though they obscure the issue by the use of Christian terms. We will speak more on this point later on.

The existentialists who deny personal immortality fall into two groups. Some adopt the outlook: "Eat, drink and be merry; for tomorrow we die." Nothing, they say, is permanent; nothing is important. So they withdraw into their own little circle of friends and live from day to day. This is the true "hippie" type. They are kind and loving in their own small circle; for this makes life easier to bear. But they refuse to become involved in the wider problems of mankind. They prefer to get away from it all—some even to a drug-induced world of dreams.

On the other side are the active existentialists. Their attitude may be described as one of "courageous despair." They acknowledge that ultimately human life is meaningless and absurd. Death is the end of individual consciousness, and it will finally be the end for all mankind. Nevertheless, while they are here on earth, they will struggle to make this a better world for themselves and for others.

According to this philosophy, the resolute man will accept his human condition with courage. He will be true to himself. Amid the bludgeonings of fate, his head will remain "bloody but unbowed." "He will dream the impossible dream; he will fight the unbeatable foe." When he goes out of life, covered with scars, if only he be true to himself, the world will be a better place because he has lived in it.

There is a movie, *Cool Hand Luke,* which expresses this philosophy with almost classic simplicity.

Luke, the central figure, is a handsome, sensitive, harmless, but highly individualistic person. By a quirk of fate, he is thrown against the establishment in one of its worst forms—in a southern chain gang. The men who run it are vicious, coldly cruel and utterly impersonal.

Poor Luke is always getting himself into trouble by his lack of conformity. At first his rebellion against the established order is good natured and easy going. It consists in little things like talking and joking with the guards or showing a playful exuberance in his work which no convict should show. However, this rebellion grows deeper and more bitter as the cold, efficient cruelty of the guards, the drab misery of prison conditions and the blows of life beat upon him.

Nevertheless, he will not give up. Nothing can break his spirit. No matter how hopeless, no matter how useless the struggle, he will still fight on. No one can make him surrender.

This is brought out in many different ways. In one scene, he is forced into a fight with a huge fellow convict. It's strictly no contest. Luke is knocked down again and again by powerful punches. But he gets up again and again! At first the other convicts are excited, calling for blood; but as battered, helpless Luke keeps getting up from the ground, they become ashamed, frightened, and beg him to stay down. Finally, even the man he is fighting pleads with him not to get up again; but he will not give in. At last, his opponent turns and walks out of the circle. Luke is left alone in the center, bloody, beaten, and yet in a sense triumphant.

He tries to escape again and again. In these attempts, he runs and runs, till his feet are like lead and his lungs are bursting. Each time he is recaptured, beaten half to death and worked to exhaustion. But he still won't give in. He escapes once more.

The climax comes in an abandoned church where he takes refuge for the night. Suddenly, the place is surrounded by police cars. He steps to the door and shouts a flippant remark to the police. At that moment, one of the prison guards shoots him in the neck. He is dumped into a police wagon and bleeds to death on the way back to prison.

The movie comes to a close with a scene of his fellow convicts gleefully agreeing: "Old Luke, he never gave in!"

Here we have all the elements of the classic existentialism of Heidegger, Sartre and Camus. The movie portrays man's anguished struggle to be himself in the difficult situations into which he is forced by a hostile world. It emphasizes the uselessness and hopelessness of this struggle. In spite of this, a brave man will face his fate with courage and resolution. He will not surrender, even though human life and, indeed, the whole universe is meaningless and absurd.

In one way or another, you will find this same theme running through existentialist novels, drama, art, and even religious literature today.

Discussion Points

1.   Why is it important for a Catholic to have an understanding of existentialism? How did the existential approach get into the modern Church? Would you be more likely to find an existentialist in a contemplative monastery or on a picket line? Why?

2.   What is existentialism? Is it a philosophical system, a religion, a movement, or what?

3.   Show how the existentialist approaches every question from the angle of the thoughts and feelings of the individual human person.

4.   In an existential catechism would you be likely to find a treatment of the nature and attributes of God? Explain your answer.

5.   Would an existentialist accept the definition of man

as a being composed of body and soul? Why not? Can you frame an existential definition of man?

6. Authority seems to be running into trouble every where—in the home, the Church, the school, civil society. Can this be traced to some degree back to the influence of existential thought?

7. Can you mention any other areas of life in which existentialism is making its influence felt?

8. Mention some of the principal existentialists and tell what you know about them.

9. What values have such men contributed to modern thought?

10. Traditional Catholic theology states that in the Eucharist the substance of the bread is changed into the substance of the body of Christ. Would an existentialist find it difficult to accept such a statement?

11. Why are existentialists so opposed to abstract ideas and principles?

12. Explain the existential meaning of the term "authentic existence."

13. Can personal immortality be reconciled with the existentialist view of man in which human consciousness is pictured as a succession of changing states without any permanent principle?

14. What is the reaction of the various existentialists to the inevitability of death? Explain Heidegger's philosophy of "courageous despair."

15. Discuss the movie *Cool Hand Luke* and show how it dramatizes the philosophy of pessimistic existentialism. Give other examples in literature and drama.

CHAPTER VI

THE IMPACT OF PERSONALISM

As we mentioned before, American Catholics as a group had very little acquaintance with the existential thinking of such men as Heidegger, Sartre and Camus. That is why many of them, including writers and theologians, seem to believe that the personalist approach to religion was born at Vatican II. This is by no means the case. It came into existence long before the Council and has a very discernible human history.

Its basic foundation, which is to treat all things from the angle of the individual human consciousness, can be traced back to the subjective philosophy of Descartes and Kant.

The application of this idea to modern life in the form of personalism has been made by the existential philosophers, as described in the last chapter. These men reject the old approach, with its emphasis on the essential and universal, the absolute and unchanging aspects of things. They want no part of a viewpoint which sees man as a creature composed of body and soul, a part of a universe in which things are endowed with specific natures, and are subject to absolute laws, both physical and moral.

The existentialists, on the contrary, are preoccupied with the concrete, individual, personal features of man's existence. For them the basic character of human life consists in change, consciousness, movement, concern, decision, in the search to find one's authentic self amid the life situations into which each person is thrown.

THREE POSSIBLE PATHS

Taking the existential view as a starting point, with reference to religion we can pursue one of three paths:

1) atheistic involvement, 2) agnostic commitment, 3) Christian encounter.

One who chooses in favor of atheism, walks with such well-known names as Jean Paul Sartre and Albert Camus. For them, all existence is meaningless and absurd. Rejecting God, they lose all possibility of finding intelligible values for human life in a divine plan. There is no "human nature," no universal design, no purpose for human life. Man is only an embodied consciousness, thrown without his consent into a world which threatens him with death. He is deeply involved in the problems of this world, pressed down by anxiety, by desires and longings, by fear and the sense of guilt. He must without guidance make his own free decisions without ever knowing whether he makes the right decisions.

There are no absolute truths, no objective moral standards, no natural law. What is right in one case may be wrong in another. Hence, in the field of morality, we arrive at what is called *situation ethics*. But, no matter what decisions we make, the end of it all, as far as any man can know, will be a universe in which there will remain only burned-out stars revolving in the blackness of unending space.

AGNOSTIC COMMITMENT

A halfway stage between atheism and religion is the agnostic commitment of Martin Heidegger and his followers. To put it briefly, in this view, man makes his way through life always committed to a resolute impotence. We simply don't know what life is all about. Consciousness is like a spark which suddenly appears in the darkness, glows for a little while, and then is extinguished. We can only guess at the meaning of life, or whether it has any meaning at all. In true German fashion, we are asked to play a Wagnerian opera role on the stage of life, a role which begins and ends in darkness and uncertainty. Doubt is the perpetual climate of the human mind.

Nevertheless, the brave man faces resolutely the uncertain future, and stands erect under the blows of fate, with head bloody but unbowed. To live amid the tragic circumstances of life with human dignity and equilibrium—here lies man's true grandeur.

CHRISTIAN ENCOUNTER

Finally, we may strive to combine existential thinking with the acceptance, in whole or in part, of the Christian faith. Of course, this can result in a tremendous number of different religious systems, according to the type of Christianity professed, and the degree to which existential thought is applied. The term "Christian existentialism" takes in doctrines as diverse as the "God is dead" theology of William Hamilton and the Roman Catholicism of Karl Rahner. Let's see if we can sort this out a bit.

BACK TO THE BEGINNING

The application of existentialist ideas to Christianity has been made chiefly by German liberal Protestant theologians. The term "liberal," or "neo-Reformed," is important here, because most of the tenets of this group are rejected by orthodox Protestants who adhere to the traditional presentation of Christian doctrine.

The beginnings of the "new theology" are often credited to Friedrich Schleiermacher, (1768-1834). Although he was not an existentialist in the modern sense of the word, he introduced the idea that religion belongs to the realm of *feeling* rather than *knowing*. This feeling grows from an immediate, intuitive, personal awareness of God's presence. Doctrines and creeds are unimportant. They are merely symbolic expressions of man's inner need for something greater and stronger than himself, recorded in the language and literature of various places and times. Thus, for instance, the dogma of original sin merely means that mankind is weak and in need of help from God. Sin is not disobedience to particular moral laws, but consists in "alienation from God." This alienation is overcome by Christ, who restores us to communion with God.

God is infinite and transcendent. Hence He cannot be known directly as He is in himself. He can be known only in man and in the world. Religion and morality are essentially social. There are no absolute moral laws. The moral behavior of each individual must be regulated by the circumstances in which he finds himself. It must be related to others: to his family, his community and the whole society in which he lives.

HARNACK

The next great name in the bridge that stretches from Kant to modern existential theology is that of Adolf von Harnack (1851-1930). By many he is held to be the greatest of all liberal Protestant theologians. According to Harnack, the essence of Christianity consists in the acceptance of God as a Father. This was perfectly perceived by Jesus Christ, who was a wise and holy man, but not divine. Jesus' whole doctrine consisted in teaching that God is our Father and all men are our brothers. The kingdom of God which He proclaimed exists merely in the hearts of men. It has no external form or organization.

Beginning with St. Paul, Harnack declares, Greek (or Hellenic) thought began to impose itself upon Christianity, and gradually set up a highly organized system of dogmatic teachings. What Harnack wanted to do, was to "dehellenize" Christianity. That is, to lop off all dogmas and doctrines, to say goodbye to all churches and creeds, and to get back to the simple, uncomplicated doctrine of Jesus, as accepted in the hearts of men of good will.

As pupils of Harnack in the university of Berlin, we find three men who, more than all others, have shaped Protestant theology as it exists today, and who have had profound influence on the "new Catholic theology." These men are: 1) Karl Barth, 2) Rudolf Bultmann and 3) Paul Tillich. We will be hearing of them frequently in succeeding pages. For it is impossible to understand developments in the Catholic Church during and since the Vatican Council without some knowledge of the works of these scholars. In fact, a good deal of the theological writing that has passed as "new" has been taken, often with little or no alteration, from Barth, Bultmann and Tillich.

GENERAL TRENDS

There are many other important names in modern liberal Protestant theology. Some of them we will meet as we go along. However, the important thing is not the names of individuals, but the recognition of the general trend of religious thought which they represent. For them, in general, Christianity does not consist in a set pattern of objective dogmas or beliefs. It is rather an encounter with God by faith, which for them is a "religious experience," a vital, immanent awareness of God. Christian beliefs are stripped of their traditional meaning; they are "demythologized." They become rather projections of man's inner religious needs than objective truths.

Among some there is an emphasis on the transcendence, the unknowability of God. Man does not come to God directly, but only through the world and through his fellow men. The important thing, they say, is to make a better world, rather than to worship God by religious cult.

MAN-CENTERED, NOT GOD-CENTERED

Religion, in other words, for them is man-centered, rather than God-centered. It is tailored to fit man's needs. The idea of God is changed to conform to what man wants, rather than making man conform to what God wants. Anything that is not considered "relevant to modern man," is tossed into the discard.

This is true likewise in the realm of morality. There is no eternal law by which God guides His creatures to the purpose for which He created them. There is no natural law by which man recognizes the will of his creator. In fact, for many the very idea of obedience to law, even the law of God, is repugnant to the dignity and freedom of man. Man determines his own morality, according to what seems best to him in the various life situations in which he finds himself. The important thing is that he follow his own conscience, a conscience subject to no law outside itself.

WHAT OF CHRIST?

Although these philosophers and theologians consider themselves "Christians," many flatly reject the divinity of Christ. They consider Him a wise, great and good man. His proclamation of the brotherhood of all men, and His invitation to "love one another," mark the path along which the social evolution of mankind can best proceed. Still, they say, in spite of His wisdom and goodness, Christ was no more than a man, and subject to all the weaknesses and temptations to which human flesh is heir. His knowledge was limited; His thought and language colored by the world view of His time.

In this process of demythologizing, they get rid of most of the traditional beliefs about Christ. The Virgin birth is nonsense. The doctrine of the union of the divine and human natures in the one Person of Christ, they say, is a sample of how Greek thought has intruded into Christian teaching. The miracles of Christ never occurred. They were simply projected backward by the faith of Christians of a later age.

In fact, some doubt whether Christ ever existed at all. Perhaps He was merely created by the faith of the early Church. At any rate, for them the question is not important. What is important is the *Kerygma,* the preaching to the world of the message of brotherhood and love, which has been attributed to Christ. It is by this message that the world will be saved, whether Christ ever lived or not.

Authority in religion or morals is for such men intolerable. Since there are no objectively true dogmas or creeds, no absolute and universal laws of morality, there can be no Church with power to tell us what we must believe or what we must do. Each man is sovereign, individual and free. It's up to him to work out for himself the system of belief and the standard of morality that suits him best.

The doctrine of the true and physical resurrection of Jesus Christ and of personal immortality for the individual believer are certainly central points in traditional Christianity. In fact, these two doctrines are very closely tied together, according to St. Paul: "If there is no resurrection of the dead, neither has Christ risen; and if Christ has not risen, vain then is our preaching, vain too is your faith" (1 Cor. 15:13). However, for liberal Protestants, such as Bultmann, Tillich and Reinhold Niebuhr, both the resurrection of Christ and of the individual believer from the dead must be taken only as symbolically, not literally true. Heaven and hell are likewise merely symbols. To consider them as states of future existence would be absurd.

CONCLUSION

What we have given here is a short summary of the

development of German liberal Protestant theology. This explanation is by no means complete. However, it will encourage us both to look for useful insights in what such men have written, and to be aware of the extremes to which their approach can lead, if it gets out of hand.

It is both interesting and instructive to note that some of the battles being fought in Catholic theology today have been going on among the Protestants for over a century. We can learn much from them.

The fundamental question which stands out in such conflicts is this: Do we begin our study of religion with God's revelation or with man's personal understanding of existence? Does theology deal with the objective nature and activity of God, as disclosed in Jesus Christ, or is its concern limited to the existential relation of man and God. In other words, is our religion going to be objective or subjective, or a combination of both?

Discussion Points

1. What was the attitude of American Catholics toward existential thought before Vatican II? What happened at the Council to change this attitude?

2. Was the personalist approach to religion born at Vatican II? Can you tell anything of its previous history?

3. Describe the atheistic involvement of Jean Paul Sartre and Albert Camus.

4. Martin Heidegger has been called the father of existentialism. What was his attitude toward religion?

5. Explain the statement that "Christian existentialism takes in doctrines as diverse as the 'God is dead' theology of William Hamilton and the Roman Catholicism of Karl Rahner?

6. What group of theologians has been chiefly responsible for introducing existentialism into Christianity? How have these ideas been received by orthodox Protestants?

7. Discuss the ideas of Schleiermacher. Why is he sometimes called the father of the new theology?

8. What did Harnack contribute to liberal Protestant theology?

9. Name some of the leaders of modern liberal Protestant theology. Summarize the general trend of religious thought which they represent. What is their attitude with regard to 1) faith; 2) worship; 3) obedience to God; 4) morality?

10. What is meant by the phrase "a man-centered religion"?

11. Explain the views of liberal Protestant writers, such as Bultmann, Tillich and Niebuhr, with regard to: 1) the divinity of Christ; 2) the virgin birth; 3) the supernatural character of the Christian religion; 4) the authority of the Church; 5) personal immortality; 6) the social doctrine of the Gospel.

12. What can Catholics learn from the century-old struggle between liberal and orthodox Protestantism? Identify some of the leading figures and the chief issues.

Chapter VII

GOD AND MODERN MAN

When man seeks to know God, he is inevitably confronted with mystery. For God is infinite and the mind of man is finite. Hence the Scripture cries out:

"Oh, the depth of the riches of the wisdom and of the knowledge of God! How incomprehensible are his judgments and how unsearchable his ways! For 'Who has known the mind of the Lord, or who has been his counselor? Or who has first given to him, that recompense should be made him?' For from him and through him and unto him are all things. To him be the glory forever, amen" (Rom. 11:33).

No human thought can contain, nor can human language express the infinity of God. To comprehend Him one would need a mind equal to that of God. Hence, when man speaks of the wonderful works of God, especially as revealed through Jesus Christ, he must do so with humility and reverence, realizing he is telling a story of wisdom, power and love too great to be fully grasped.

But does this mean that we can know nothing at all of God? Some have adopted this position.

THE AGNOSTICS

The question of man's knowledge of God is intimately bound up with the wider problem of the nature of human knowledge. Can man know anything outside his own mind? Can he know things as they really are, or only as they appear to him? To put it popularly, can we "get behind the looking glass"? In particular, can we know invisible and spiritual realities?

As we have seen, some philosophers deny that man

can know anything but his own thoughts. Logically, then, they must also deny that man can really know God. That is, unless they identify God with the human mind, as do the pantheistic idealists.

It is also clear that anyone who claims the only valid form of knowledge is sense knowledge, must also hold that man cannot know God. For God is invisible and spiritual. He cannot be seen by the eyes or grasped by the senses.

The position that man cannot know God because he cannot be certain there is any reality behind the phenomena presented to him by his senses is called "agnosticism." This term is derived from the Greek word which means "unknowing." Developed by such men as Herbert Spencer and August Comte in the nineteenth century, agnosticism is still the attitude toward God professed by many "intellectuals" today. It is, moreover, the staple religious fare now being served to students on most college campuses.

EMPTYING THE CONCEPT OF GOD

Under the guise of "making God relevant to modern man," there is a movement afoot to empty the concept of God of all, or almost all, its traditional content. When we examine this tendency, we find that it is merely another manifestation of the subjectivism and relativism which is cropping up everywhere in modern thought.

This rejection of traditional Christian doctrines began among the liberal Protestants. Leaders in the movement were Adolf von Harnack, Albrecht Ritschl and Ernst Troeltsch. Only recently have such ideas appeared in Catholic publications. Perhaps the clearest expression of this tendency is found in *The Future of Belief,* by Leslie Dewart.

Strange to say, this book has received considerable acclaim among Catholics. It is doubtful, however, whether some of those who have praised the book really understood what it is all about.

Let it be said that it is no disgrace not to find this book crystal clear at first reading. In order to interpret it correctly, one must have some knowledge of the writings of Paul Tillich, Rudolf Bultmann, Dietrich Bonhoeffer, Martin Heidegger, Roger Garaudy, Edmund Husserl, Gabriel Marcel, and a dozen other contemporary or near contemporary philosophers and theologians.

One would also have to possess a fairly extensive knowledge of the writings of St. Thomas Aquinas to be able to check Dewart's many direct and indirect attacks on him. Finally, much of the book would remain dark to one who had little knowledge of either ancient Greek philosophy or the Hebrew outlook of Biblical days.

This does not mean that we should naively accept Dewart's statements as being too erudite to be questioned. Actually, there is very little that is new or original in the ideas which he advances. Almost all can be traced back to the writers mentioned above, particularly to Harnack and Tillich.

We shall examine what Dewart says: 1) about the mode and expression of man's knowledge of God; 2) about the nature of God.

MAN'S KNOWLEDGE OF GOD

We present three direct quotations from *The Future of Belief* as a summary of Dewart's position.

"This book advances, first, the suggestion that the integration of Christian belief and contemporary experience must logically begin—that is, it cannot in the end abstract from—the integration of the *concept of God* with contemporary experience" (p. 37).

"More concretely, it will be suggested that the integration of theism with today's everyday experience requires not merely the *demythologization of Scripture* but the more comprehensive *dehellenization of dogma,* and specifically that of the Christian doctrine of God" (p. 49).

"This would in turn imply that Christian theism should first become conscious that its traditional form has necessarily and logically been childish and infantile to the very degree that it corresponded to an earlier, relatively childish infantile stage of human evolution" (p. 51).

What Dewart is saying is simply this: "Traditional expressions of Christian doctrine, especially about God, are childish and infantile. They are such because they were produced by ignorant and underdeveloped cultures (Hebrew and Greek). They must be totally reformed to be acceptable to modern man."

WHO IS MODERN MAN?

Dewart is continually speaking of "modern man." By this he means not the mass of humanity, but a relatively small group of philosophers who deny that man can obtain absolute truth. These he identifies with "contemporary man," and he makes their outlook the criterion of all truth. Anything which he feels does not square with "contemporary experience" is rejected without further argument. He seems to have no suspicion that the type of subjective and relative philosophy which he has adopted may itself be the result of an incorrect understanding of the nature of human knowledge and of the manner in which the mind attains truth.

In his process of adjusting traditional Christian thinking to "contemporary experience," Dewart advances two ideas which he considers fundamental to his program. The first of these is the *demythologizing of the Bible.* The meaning of this idea, which has been borrowed from Bultmann, will be explained more in detail later on. What Dewart means is that everything which the Bible says about God is expressed in the language of myth. To get at the real meaning, we must, he says, strip away all these old myths.

Secondly, he demands the *dehellenizing of theology*. This concept, which can be traced back to Harnack, is based on the assumption that St. Paul and others introduced ideas from Greek philosophy into early Christianity. All these Greek elements, Dewart says, must be removed from theology.

What Dewart actually arrives at in his book is a *deconceptualizing* of God. One by one, he rejects all the ideas which have been traditionally associated with the name of God. At last, there remains only an empty word—a God who cannot be loved or worshipped because He can in no way be conceived by human thought or expressed in human language.

The first important criticism that must be leveled at Dewart, therefore, is this: instead of boldly admitting that he has adopted the views of one particular group of philosophers and theologians, he writes as if these views were today universally accepted and beyond all dispute among intelligent people.

This is not the case. There are expressions of truth concerning God's revelation of himself to mankind which remain eternally true through all the cultural changes to which human society is subject. Such are, for instance, the simple statements of the Creed which are just as meaningful for modern man as they were to Christians of the first century: "I believe in one God, the Father almighty, Creator of heaven and earth . . . and in Jesus Christ, His Son . . . I believe in the holy Catholic Church, the forgiveness of sins, the resurrection of the body and life everlasting."

We needn't be concerned that a certain number of sophisticated intellectuals reject the Christian message as being too simple and naive for their acceptance. St.

Paul ran into the very same mentality among the Greeks, who likewise had their skeptics. We find his rejection of the so-called "wisdom" of man as the criterion of divine truth in the powerful passage:

"Has not God turned to foolishness the 'wisdom' of this world? For since, in God's wisdom, the world did not come to know God by 'wisdom,' it pleased God, by the foolishness of our preaching, to save those who believe. For the Jews asked for signs, and the Greeks looked for 'wisdom'; but we, for our part, preach a crucified Christ—to the Jews indeed a stumbling block and to the Gentiles foolishness, but to those who are called, both Jews and Greeks, Christ, the power of God and the wisdom of God. For the foolishness of God is wiser than men, and the weakness of God is stronger than men" (1 Cor. 1:20).

Christianity can never be pleasing to the "contemporary mind" of any age if this mind is marked by intellectual pride, self-sufficiency and independence. For, as Christ pointed out, only those who become docile and humble like little children can enter His kingdom.

A WORLD COME OF AGE

Dewart sneers at the wisdom of the past and declares it childish and infantile. He subtitles his book "Theism in a World Come of Age."

However, when we look at the real world around us, with its turmoil and its problems, we wonder how he could speak in such optimistic terms of the state of humanity. Man has, indeed, made tremendous strides in the physical sciences; but he has not made a comparable advance in wisdom.

A huge proportion of the human race is still tormented by hunger and poverty. Linked with these are other problems among the poor: miserable, overcrowded housing, wretched living and working conditions, and illiteracy. Even in the developed nations, cities are confronted with the problem of vast slum areas which are the spawning ground for crime, juvenile delinquency and other forms of human degradation. When the race element is added, the situation becomes even more explosive, erupting at times in uncontrolled riots.

Hanging like a pall over mankind is the fear of a nuclear war which would reduce everything to ashes. The very science of which modern man is so proud threatens, like a frankenstein, to destroy him who made it.

Realizing that the ills which beset humanity—poverty, hunger, illiteracy, racial injustice and war—are of man's own making, how can anyone call this "a world come of age"? Or maintain that modern man has no need of God because he can now solve his own problems?

ATTEMPT AT REBUILDING

Like Descartes and Kant before him, Dewart conceives his work as consisting of two parts: 1) tearing down the old, 2) building up the new. However, like Descartes and Kant, the "new" seems to consist of a religious subjectivism, based on an inner experience, which few are likely to accept, any more than they accepted the "clear ideas" of Descartes or the "imperative command of conscience" of Kant.

Dewart attempts: 1) to tear down the traditional concept of God; 2) to reconstruct a new theism.

However, the foundation of this reconstruction is purely subjective, an interpretation of an inner personal experience which may, or may not, be verified in the consciousness of others. It is certainly a very flimsy foundation upon which to try to reconstruct the whole of Christian doctrine.

Dewart himself recognizes the shakiness of his foundation: "On the working assumption of the diagnosis made above, that Christianity suffers from absolute theism, the question arises: Once Christianity becomes fully conscious of the need for further developing its theism, how is it likely to reconceptualize consciously its belief in God? Nowhere in this essay would I want to stress the tentative and exploratory character of my remarks more than in my attempt to answer this question" (p. 171).

He suggests that in the future Christians will not conceive of God as a *being,* not even a *super-being.* God, according to him, does not exist; He is beyond essence and existence. Indeed, he says, Christians may in the future not conceive God as a person—or indeed as a Trinity of persons. Nor is He suprapersonal.

Dewart rejects all the traditional attributes of God. He is not all-powerful, eternal, immaterial, infinite, unchangeable or all-knowing. We are not to think of God's providence guiding the world according to a plan. God does not even know the direction in which the evolution of the world is proceeding.

According to him, if we ask whether God can make a blind man see, the dead to rise again, or a virgin to conceive—it is not less misleading to answer yes than to answer no. It is childish, he declares, to believe that miracles can happen, including "the miracle of the glorious return of the Christ upon a cloud." Any future direction of the course of evolution will be the responsibility of man. "Unless we make it be, the kingdom of God shall never come."

Dewart goes on to say that man's future understanding of religion will probably exclude any idea of obedience or worship paid to God. He says:

"As Christian theism is dehellenized, the Christian faith may recast the meaning of religion in terms that do not *at all* imply God's ascendency over man, or man's submission to God" (p. 200).

"I think that the Christian theism of the future might so conceive God as to find it possible to look back with amusement on the day when it was thought particularly appropriate that the believer should bend his knee in order to worship God" (p. 203).

Dewart, following a theme found frequently in Tillich, ridicules the idea that the final end of Christian life consists in happiness found in the possession of God. Although he does not state this directly, he seems to reject any idea of personal immortality. This, he implies, would not be attuned to "contemporary experience" (p. 28-36).

The alternative for him consists in man's striving not *to be happy,* but *to be.* In other words, we are back to the search for the authentic self and to the courageous despair of Heidegger.

ANYTHING POSITIVE?

We have investigated the negative side of Dewart's presentation. Certainly it leaves little or nothing of what men have hitherto conceived of as God. In fact, Dewart would be quite willing to get rid of the name "God" altogether (p. 212). Does he replace this with anything positive?

For him, as is to be expected, God is not to be found in the world, but in *the consciousness of man.* He is not there as anything known, but as a *presence.* This idea, taken from Gabriel Marcel, is substantiated only by an appeal to inner experience. Because this is an experience of something that is not evident, it takes on the character of *belief,* or *faith.* He declares:

"The ordinary facts of Christian experience are sufficient to establish that we do *experience* God, but that we do not experience Him as *being.* This proposition should be obvious and commonplace to the philosophically unprejudiced Christian believer. In fact, since it is a matter of simple observation it should be one of the starting points of Christian philosophical inquiry. . . . God is, among other ways in which we can conceptualize the matter, that which we experience as the open background of consciousness and being" (p. 175).

But, it may be asked, is it true that men have such an inner experience of God as present to them? Or is this a purely personal interpretation of the facts of human consciousness resulting from Dewart's Christian background? He admits that what he says is not capable of proof:

"I should underline that the 'proof' I have suggested above not only has nothing to say about God's 'existence' properly so called, but that it is hardly a proof in the classical sense of the term. It concerns a reality which is not the object of any actual or possible empirical intuition. Therefore, it is an essentially *unverifiable* argument. It is always possible to look at the same facts and find nothing but the *absence* of God. This is why I have formulated the argument in hypothetical form" (p. 178).

We're back on the old familiar grounds of subjectivism. Like Descartes and Kant, Dewart has tried to tear down the old structure of man's knowledge of God. He has gotten rid of the God of the Old Testament and the New, the God men have known and loved and worshipped for thousands of years. For this God of the Bible and of the Church, he has nothing to substitute except an unverifiable, purely subjective interpretation of God as "the open background of consciousness and being."

The sad thing is, that many persons may accept Dewart's work of destruction, but reject his rather flimsy attempts at reconstruction, and thus be left without any idea of God at all.

Discussion Points

1. Why is man confronted with mystery when he seeks to know God? Can the mind of man grasp the totality of God in a single concept? Explain that man must combine many ideas, such as power, goodness, truth and love, to arrive at the fullest possible concept of God.

2. Does the fact we cannot know everything about God mean that we cannot know anything of God? Explain briefly how we can know God: 1) in creation; 2) through Jesus Christ.

3. What is agnosticism? Show how this logically follows from: 1) subjectivism, which denies that man can know objective truth; 2) positivism, which denies that man can know anything which cannot be grasped by sense knowledge.

4. Discuss the relationship between Christian revelation and the "contemporary mind" of each succeeding generation of mankind. Can the contemporary viewpoint be made a criterion for judging truth? What concessions can and should be made to the viewpoint of the age?

5. Describe St. Paul's reaction to the statement of Greek intellectuals that Christianity is too childish and naive for acceptance (cf. 1 Cor. 1:8-2:16).

6. Is it true that the traditional concept of God, as Creator, Father, Protector, Friend, has lost its meaning and relevance for intelligent men today?

7. Identify the steps which Dewart takes in "integrating theism with contemporary experience." Show how he eliminates not only all Greek ideas, but also all Hebrew ideas, and even all human ideas about God.

8. If Dewart's thesis is accepted, would it be possible for God to make an objective revelation of himself to mankind? What then happens to the Bible and the Church?

9. How do the moral, spiritual and religious problems of man today differ from those of his ancestors? To what extent is the literature of the past, such as the Bible and the works of Shakespeare, applicable to human nature today?

10. Summarize Dewart's attempt to reconstruct a new theism. What kind of God does he suggest? Does he accept any of the traditional attributes of God? What then is left?

11. What is Dewart's concept of the final purpose of human life?

12. Show the connection between Dewart's thesis and subjective and relative philosophy. Has the statement any meaning to you that "we experience God as the open background of consciousness and being"?

13. Can one build a religion for mankind on a subjective experience of the "presence" of God, which may also be experienced as an "absence" of God? Compare Dewart's attempt to reconstruct theism with the similar attempts of Descartes and Kant.

14. How can one explain the fact that *The Future of Belief* has been acclaimed by a number of Catholic journalists and writers?

CHAPTER VIII

ARE WE SECULARIZING RELIGION?

We're hearing a great deal these days about "crises of identity" among Catholics of all classes.

A young priest stands up before a congregation and, to the amazement and consternation of those present, says: "I no longer know what it means to be a priest."

A Sister—indeed, in some cases groups of Sisters—leaves the convent, explaining that she cannot fulfill her identity as a modern woman within the structure of religious life.

Reports are circulated that certain young priests no longer want to hear confessions, give out Communions, or conduct religious services because they are too busy with various forms of social action.

In a similar spirit, not a few Sisters have abandoned their traditional work of teaching and nursing in order, as they say, "to get out into the market place."

BENEATH THE SURFACE

The controversies swirling around the statements and attitudes described above—and many other examples could be quoted—indicate that there is a much deeper problem hidden here than might at first be suspected. In fact, in its deepest implications, this question can be said to be the most fundamental which concerns the relationship between God and modern man. The problem can be expressed from many different points of view.

IS GOD RELEVANT?

Probably the most common way this problem is presented today is to ask the existentialist question: Is God relevant for modern man? Those who ask this question are not interested in an analysis of the nature and attributes of God. They simply want to know whether belief in God does anything to better human life, primarily in the field of social action. Does religion help solve the civil rights question, or effect the just distribution of property? If not, they say, "Let's get rid of it!"

RELIGIOUS OR SOCIAL MISSION?

Another way to look at this problem is to ask: Is the primary mission of the Church religious or social? How far is it the duty of the Church to work for the temporal betterment of mankind? Should she intervene by direct action? Or should she act indirectly by guiding men toward correct moral and social attitudes? Since effective results in this sphere to a great extent depend on political action, to what extent should the Church enter the arena of politics and seek to influence politicians? Should the Church use her economic power to enforce moral viewpoints?

NUNS IN PICKET LINES?

To put the matter a little more concretely, we may ask: "What is a priest? What is a religious?" Some would answer: Primarily a priest is a man with the power and duty to offer Mass, to administer the sacraments, and to break the bread of God's word to the people. A religious is a man or woman completely dedicated to God's service by membership in an institute with a specific religious purpose approved by the Church.

An existentialist would reply: "A priest or a religious is a man or woman 'for others.'" The emphasis would be not on the religious aspect of the priesthood or religious life, but on the service such persons can render to their fellow men, particularly by contributing toward a solution of the burning problems of the day, such as war and peace and racial tension. From this point of view, one can understand the urge to leave the classroom or the pulpit for the picket line or the peace march. The agony for such persons comes when they ask: "What can I do in this way 'for others,' that I could not do better if I were not a priest or religious? Could I not work more effectively in secular garb, without the restrictions of obedience, unhampered by religious duties?"

A more theological phrasing of the question would be: Can I know and love God directly in himself or only in my fellow man? Does the whole of religion consist in loving one's neighbor? Is it possible for a human being to approach God directly, to love God as one person loves another, to enter into any kind of union with God? Or can we find God only in our neighbor, so that the only conceivable religious obligations we have are those of doing good to our fellow men? To what degree is religion simply and solely humanitarianism?

Perhaps the simplest, yet most profound, way to present this fundamental problem is to ask: Should religion be God-centered or man-centered? Should we build cathedrals and spend time and effort in the worship of God? Or should we forget all that and concentrate on building houses and schools for the underprivileged?

To the questions above, all of which to some extent center around the same basic problem, a wide variety of answers are given today. The character of these answers, will, of course, depend upon the basic religious outlook and convictions of those who present them. Let's examine and try to weigh the merits of the various answers.

THE ATHEIST-AGNOSTIC ANSWER

We group the atheist and agnostic here, because in

practice their answer boils down to the same thing. The fundamental premise of such persons consists in the denial that God exists or that we can know anything about Him if He does exist. The only practical reality, in their view, is to be found in things which a man can touch, see, hear, smell, and observe and experiment with under physically controlled conditions.

Often, but not always, the atheist-agnostic makes a kind of religion out of humanism, out of concern for his fellow man. He takes the position that he himself will be happier, and the world will become a better place in which to live if he tries to prevent or alleviate human suffering wherever it confronts his sensibilities. He is concerned that something be done about poverty and slums and human hunger and race prejudice and war and over-population. He sees the suffering caused by these circumstances, and is against it on principle, and often in generous action as well.

The humanists, therefore, hold that true religion consists only in concern for one's fellow man. Their religion has, however, one terrifying weakness: it is based on no rational foundation. If human life has no ultimate destiny, if everything is meaningless and absurd, why should we be particularly concerned about our fellow men? Take, for instance, a slave in ancient Rome. What does it matter now whether he was happy or unhappy, whether he experienced pleasure or pain, joy or sorrow, hunger or plenty? He's as dead as the ant which we trample thoughtlessly under foot and, without God, his life has no more importance.

The position of the atheist-agnostic possesses no principles, no unchangeable guidelines about human nature. Rejecting the spiritual nature of man, it undermines the whole structure of human rights.

Hence his concern for his fellow man becomes nothing more than a matter of feeling or sentiment, subject to the instability that has always characterized human feeling.

THE ANSWER OF THE "CONFUSED CHRISTIAN"

Vatican Council II, especially in its *Constitution on the Church in the Modern World,* emphasized strongly the duty of Christians to help build a better world. This admonition has been interpreted by some as meaning that man is called to know and love God only through his fellow man. Religion, they say, should be "horizontal," that is, extending itself upon the earth, rather than "vertical," that is, trying to reach from earth to heaven. Action is more important than prayer. Indeed, the only true prayer consists in working for the welfare of one's fellow man.

This position had already been popularized by a number of Protestant writers, even before the Council. The high priest of this group is Dietrich Bonhoeffer. This man had a very unusual life which ended in his execution by the Nazis shortly before the conclusion of World War II. During his whole life, up to the last ten months, he had been a devout orthodox Protestant minister. Because of his secret anti-Nazi activities, he was caught and imprisoned.

What happened to him in prison, we shall probably never know. The only record we have of that period is from letters he wrote to friends. In these, he shows himself increasingly more despondent. The burden of his message is: "We have long waited for God to free us from the Nazi evil; but He has not come. Now we must take things into our own hands and strive to make a better world for mankind." He developed a type of secularized, or "religionless Christianity." Christ was not divine, but was "the man for others," leading them not toward eternal life, but toward a better life on earth.

This secularized Christianity has profoundly affected the modern religious scene. It has been popularized in such books as Bishop Robinson's *Honest to God* and *The Secular City* by Harvey Cox.

Repercussions of this doctrine among Catholics have been quite extensive since the Council. While not actually going so far as to profess a "religionless Christianity," some confused Catholics have been deceived into making light of the strictly religious actions that pertain to man's direct relationship to God. They do not exactly deny that man can relate directly to God. Rather, they maintain and stress that he should concern himself far more seriously about relating to his fellow man and the world.

This is a difficult matter to treat because it is so easy, in discussing it, to *seem* to be making light of the supremely important Christian obligation of fraternal charity and to be recommending a withdrawal from the world that would amount to an escape from a duty. All such escapism from the world we soundly condemn; but we must also condemn every tendency toward escapism from God.

The latter tendency appears in many forms. The first is that of minimizing the value and effectiveness of prayer. You hear it said that action, or involvement, or bearing witness, or penetration of the world, is the best form of prayer. The inference is that extricating oneself from the world once in a while for the sake of prayer is a mistake; that it is self-deception, because you don't really enter into communion with God, but you merely escape the problems and battles of life under the pretext of prayer. It is also said that the only kind of prayer that is worth anything consists in Christian witness to the world of love for others.

This leads quite logically into a downgrading of the age-old practices of meditation and contemplation.

These familiar forms of prayer are usually not condemned outright. But they are made to seem a little suspect, or less than fruitful and effective, a far cry from the "highest possible form of human activity," which is charitable action.

This genteel disparagement of prayer and contemplation leads to the thinly veiled position that the three vows of the religious life no longer possess the tremendous value, as self-offerings to God, that centuries of Christian living have given them. Again there is a hint that it is no longer "in" to direct one's attention to God. The world needs and demands all our attention now.

To make a vow of poverty, therefore, is rather foolish because it means giving up control over things that can be used to help others. To make a vow of chastity is both damaging to personality and idle and empty, because everything in the world is important, and the use of sex is one of the most important things of all. Finally, to make a vow of obedience means giving up the one thing, freedom, that is most valuable in dealing with the world.

Thus the confused Catholic finds himself more at home with the "God is unreachable" kind of Christian than with other Catholics. Sometimes he seems to retire even to the position of the agnostic humanist, so far from God that he is beginning to wonder why a fuss is being made by some of his fellow Catholics over such matters as divorce and remarriage, sterilization, homosexuality, abortion, etc.

THE ANSWER OF FAITH AND REASON

The documents of Vatican II do, indeed, stress unequivocally the duties of Christians to work for a better world. The *Constitution on the Church in the Modern World,* states explicitly: "Far from turning us away from our earthly task, our adhesion to Christ in faith commits us totally to the service of our brethren." This theme has been developed at length in Volume VIII of this Catholic Living Series, *Making A Better World with Vatican II.*

However, this, and other similar statements, cannot be construed as meaning that the individual human being has no personal and direct relationship to God or that he can approach God only through his fellow man. Out of many possible citations from Vatican II, a few will suffice to make this point abundantly clear.

1) In the *Constitution on the Church in the Modern World,* where, if any place, the Council might have seemed to be more concerned with man's relation to his fellow man than with his relation to God, the basis for every single practical recommendation is set down as *man's personal relationship to God.* It declares:

"The root reason for human dignity lies in man's call to communion with God. From the very circumstance of his origin man is already invited to converse with God. For man would not exist were he not created by God's love and constantly preserved by it; and he cannot live fully according to the truth unless he freely acknowledges that love and devotes himself to his Creator."

2) The entire *Declaration on Religious Freedom* issued by the Council bases itself squarely on the principle that man, being the image and likeness of God through the possession of a spiritual mind and the gift of free will, has an obligation to seek God, and when found, to adore Him, to love Him, and to serve Him without interference or coercion from others.

3) The *Constitution on the Liturgy* clearly answers anyone who has been led to think that action in the world is more important than prayer before God. Its primary purpose is to direct the public forms of worship to God in the Church into updated and meaning-

ful channels. But in the midst of stressing public worship, it reiterates man's need and duty of constant private communication with God. It says:

"The spiritual life is not limited solely to participation in the liturgy. The Christian is indeed called to pray with his brethren, but he must also enter into his chamber to pray to the Father in secret; yet more, according to the teaching of the apostle, he should pray without ceasing."

4) The *Decree on the Missions* develops the theme that every human being in the world needs the knowledge of God, the redemption of Christ, and all the means of union with God which Christ entrusted to His Church. Its urgent call to missionary activity leaves no doubt that the Christian is called to work for the spiritual, as well as the temporal welfare of his neighbor.

Finally, this same decree rebukes once and for all those confused Christians who have been deceived into thinking that the time has come to abandon contemplation and prayer in favor of action in the world. It says:

"Institutes of the contemplative life, by their prayers, sufferings, and works of penance, have a very great importance in the conversion of souls, because it is God who sends workers into His harvest when He is asked to do so, God who opens the minds of non-Christians to hear the Gospel, and God who fructifies the Word of salvation in their hearts."

CONCLUSION

To summarize what has been said: 1) There cannot be the slightest doubt about the duty of each Christian to work for the welfare of his fellow man. This law of fraternal charity is brought out repeatedly in the New Testament. 2) However, neither can there be any doubt that each man is called to know and love God directly and to approach Him in spirit by prayer and worship.

Christ neatly summed up the relationship between the love and service of God and of one's fellow man when He said: *Thou shalt love the Lord thy God with thy whole heart and with thy whole soul, and with thy whole mind, and with thy whole strength.* This is the first commandment. And the second is like it. *Thou shalt love thy neighbor as thyself* (Mark 12:30).

Discussion Points

1. To what extent does the "crisis of identity" affecting various types of Catholics reflect a crisis about the very nature of the Christian religion?

2. What can a priest or Sister possibly mean when they say: "I don't know what it means to be a priest, or a nun"?

3. Can the present problems of mankind—war and peace, civil rights, poverty, etc.—be solved by science? Or are they fundamentally moral problems which can be settled only in accordance with religious principles? Explain.

4. Is the primary mission of the Church religious or social? How far should the Church get involved in working for the temporal betterment of mankind? Should the Church enter politics in order to produce needed social change? Is the primary work of a priest or nun to work for the moral and spiritual betterment of men, or for improving their social and economic welfare? How can these two sides be balanced in the life of an individual?

5. Sister Alpha says: "I don't want to teach religion in a school. I want to get out and work for Christ in the market place." What advice would you give her?

6. Can we know and love God directly in himself or only in our fellow men? Should we build churches and

spend time and effort in the worship of God? Or should we concentrate all our attention on building houses and schools for the underprivileged?

7. What is humanism? Point out the fundamental weakness of agnostic and atheistic humanism. Show how ultimately human life has dignity and importance only in relation to God.

8. Comment on the statement: "The only true prayer consists in working for the welfare of one's fellow man."

9. To what degree are such statements a rebellion against the type of religion that consists entirely in pious practices, often with indifference or injustice to one's neighbor?

10. Mr. & Mrs. Zeta make a great show of being pillars of the Church. However, they pay starvation wages to their servants. Do they actually harm the cause of Christ?

11. Tell what you know about Dietrich Bonhoeffer and his "religionless Christianity." What did he mean by Christ being "a man for others"? What has been the effect of this doctrine on the attitude of some Catholics toward practices of prayer and devotion and the three vows of the religious life?

12. Explain the attitude of Vatican II toward the problem of the relationship between the sacred and the secular.

13. What does the statement mean that "the root reason for human dignity and for all man's rights lies in the fact that he is called to personal union with God"?

14. Do institutes of the contemplative life have any function in the Church today?

15. What is the difference between Christian charity and philanthropy? Show how each is based on a totally different philosophy of the nature and destiny of man, and of the relationship between the natural and the supernatural.

UNIT II

Chapter IX

CHRISTIANITY WITHOUT CHRIST

For almost 2,000 years Jesus Christ has been a controversial figure. This need occasion no surprise, since even at His birth Simeon spoke the prophecy: "Behold, this child is destined for the fall and for the rise of many in Israel, and for a sign that shall be contradicted" (Luke 2:34).

Jesus himself put the question clearly and without equivocation: "What think you of Christ? Whose Son is He?" (Matt. 22:42)

The answer to this question split the Jewish world of His time in two, and today it is beginning to divide the Christian world.

Some answer with Peter: "Thou art the Christ, the Son of the living God" (Matt. 16:16). For such as these, Christ is the "Word made flesh," the incarnate Son of God sent into the world by the Father's merciful love, to redeem all men from their sins and to unite them to himself by imparting the gift of divine life.

On the other side are those who declare that such a view is too simple and naive for the "contemporary mind." Christ, they say, if He ever lived at all, could not have been divine. He could not have been more than a man, albeit a great and wise and noble man. Still, it is admitted, He has given us the key to the world's future progress in His doctrine of fraternal love, of the brotherhood of all men. It is by "faith" in Him, by acceptance of this message, that we will find authentic self-fulfillment and courageously work for a better world here on earth, since there is no supernatural life to which we can aspire.

The present controversy about Christ swirls chiefly about the figure of the German scholar, Rudolf Bultmann. We cannot possibly understand the direction of recent New Testament studies without some knowledge of what Bultmann has written concerning: 1) the demythologizing of Scripture; 2) form criticism; 3) the *kerygma*. We will try to explain what is meant by each of these ideas and some of the effects they have had both on Protestant and Catholic Biblical studies.

Before we begin, we must recognize that Bultmann himself is a highly controversial figure among Protestants. There are some who blow him up to heroic proportions as the one chiefly responsible for bringing Christianity up-to-date and making it acceptable to the contemporary mind.

Others see in his ideas the seeds of the destruction of all true Christianity, the beginning of a perverted rationalistic religion which can lead men only to nihilism and despair.

DEMYTHOLOGIZING

Central to Bultmann's presentation of Christianity is the contention that the true message of the Gospel is hidden under a cloak of myths and symbols. Modern scientific man, he says, cannot possibly accept such myths and symbols as literally true. Hence we must strip them away and try to find the meaning concealed beneath them.

Such a program would not sound very radical if it were merely an attempt to interpret ancient modes of language and expression, to correct old views concerning the make-up of the earth and the heavens, or to remind us that the Bible is not teaching science.

However, Bultmann goes far beyond this. He rejects the whole body of what has hitherto been considered Christian doctrine, the whole of the Nicene and Apostles' Creed. When he finishes, the concept of Christ is just as empty as the concept of God presented by Tillich and Dewart. This is not immediately evident in his writings, as he continues to use Christian terms. But it is clear from a deeper analysis of his thought and language.

Everything that makes up Christianity for the ordinary Catholic or Protestant is tossed out. According to traditional Christian doctrine, man's salvation was planned in the mind of an eternal, omnipotent, merciful God. In His love, He sent His Son to redeem mankind from sin. He has power over nature, working miracles which are signs that He has come from God. He dies on the cross to atone for men's sins. He rises from the dead and ascends into heaven. From there He will come at the end of time to judge all men and to reward or punish each according to his works. According to Bultmann, none of this is literally true; it is all mythological.

Upon what does Bultmann base his rejection of Jesus Christ as the centuries have known Him, and his attempt to build up a new Christianity which has been demythologized? It is founded on his conception of "the mind of contemporary man." This for him means the outlook of those who have accepted a subjective and relative philosophy patterned on that of Martin Heidegger. Incidentally, Bultmann knew Heidegger personally and acknowledged how greatly he had been influenced by him.

In his process of demythologizing the New Testament, Bultmann begins with the rejection of the supernatural. For him it is unthinkable that God can influence nature or nature's laws from without.

By this principle, he gets rid of huge sections of the New Testament at one stroke. Christ cannot be the pre-existing Word of God. His birth cannot be foretold. It is ridiculous to think that He was born of a virgin. He can work no miracles, utter no prophecies, cast out no demons. If Jesus Christ ever lived, which is probable but not certain for Bultmann, He was subject to all the weaknesses and limitations of human nature, to the errors and superstitions of His time. His death had no atoning power; nor could He rise from the dead. Without further ado, we can thus rid ourselves of any idea of the truth of the gospel stories concerning His resurrection, His ascension, or His return as Judge. All these imply the intervention of divine power in the world; hence automatically, according to Bultmann, they must be false.

FORM CRITICISM

Bultmann does not reject entirely the idea that the gospels tell us something of the life of Jesus Christ. He agrees that probably there is a very little bit, a thin substratum, which scientific investigation can discover. In order to arrive at this, it is necessary to use the method called "form criticism." This method, to which Bultmann contributed greatly, is a tool much used by Scripture scholars today.

Form criticism looks upon the gospels not as having been written by a single author at a particular time, but as an expression of the faith of the early Christian community. This was recorded by many different persons at different times, before it was finally put together in the New Testament as we have it today. The exponents of form criticism claim to be able, by the use of certain rules, to be able to distinguish the earlier from the later traditions of the early Church. In this way, they assert, one can get back to the earliest layer which contains the actual, or close to the actual, words and deeds of Jesus.

HISTORY NOT IMPORTANT

When Bultmann's particular method of form criticism, with its denial of the supernatural, is applied to the gospels, there remains little or nothing of the historical Jesus. This does not bother Bultmann at all. For him the historical events in the life of Christ are of no importance. It does not really matter whether Jesus ever really lived on earth at all.

THE KERYGMA

Why? Because for him the words and actions of Christ have no supernatural value. Nothing that Jesus said or did could save the world. There is no objective salvation history.

However, salvation does come to man by faith in the kerygma, the proclamation of the gospel message that Jesus died and rose again. It makes no difference that this faith may have no objective historical foundation.

Here we see again the strange subjective twist of his theology, his preoccupation with things as they are in the mind of man, rather than in themselves.

There can be no doubt that this is what Bultmann means. His own repeated declarations, as well as the explicit statements of theologians who have read and interpreted his difficult writings make this abundantly clear.

For him it is man's faith in the kerygma, not the truth of the kerygma that is important. To put it in another way, it is the proclamation of the saving event of Jesus Christ, and not true statements about Him, which is the core of the Biblical message. This is what we arrive at after the New Testament has been demythologized. The event of Christ, he says, is not open to historical investigation, but only to faith. This faith is founded on nothing outside itself. It needs no base in reason or in history. It follows, therefore, that it is not the resurrection of Christ which engenders faith, but it is faith which engenders the resurrection.

REBUILDING

At this point, the average reader will ask: "Doesn't this destroy Christianity? What's the good of faith in something that isn't true?"

If Bultmann's process of demythologizing is accepted, with its rejection of everything supernatural, everything objective and historical, then we must certainly say goodbye to traditional Christianity. As a historical figure, Jesus might have for us some shadowy, vaguely discernible reality. As the Son of God, sent to save the world, He would be merely a product of man's own mind.

However, Bultmann, in his own opinion, has torn down only to rebuild. He wants to present a picture of Christianity that is acceptable to the "contemporary mind."

THE ALTERNATIVE

But what has he to offer as a substitute for traditional Christianity? When we follow him on this part of his journey, we find ourselves in the same bleak desert to which the other followers of pessimistic existentialism have led us. The only difference is that Bultmann clothes the dry bones of pessimism with Christian Biblical terms. He speaks of salvation, of Jesus Christ as a saving event, of fallen man, of the Spirit of God, of revelation. However, all these terms have for him a special meaning which is completely different from the traditional Christian meaning. To put it briefly, what Bultmann gives us is a total reinterpretation of Christianity according to a particular type of rationalistic philosophy.

This comes out quite clearly, for instance, in his concept of sin. Sin does not consist in a moral transgression, a violation of the law of God. For him, as for many existentialists, sin is the refusal to accept one's human condition of having been thrown into the world without one's choice, without security in the present, or any guarantees for the future. For him it is a "sin" to try to escape from this uncertainty of life by setting up a pre-established order. For by seeking security and certainty man is getting away from his authentic self, from what he really is.

Without help, Bultmann declares, no man would have sufficient strength or courage to divorce himself from this sinful seeking for security and certainty. This help he can receive only by faith, by accepting the kerygma that Jesus died and rose again. For in His death and resurrection we recognize Jesus' complete *openness to the future.*

A man who seeks his authentic self must renounce the security which a mythological understanding of religion gives him. He must realize that the Christian faith affords no security in this life, nor certainty of any life beyond this world. But it does give man freedom and courage to face darkness and mystery in confidence, and to accept responsibility for action in the loneliness of his own decision.

From what we have studied before, we can recognize that this is pure Heidegger presented in Christian terms! Bultmann's faith is not truly faith at all, but rationalistic and naturalistic commitment. To one who breaks beneath the surface of language, it is evident that Bultmann's doctrine is a complete distortion of Christianity.

CATHOLIC BIBLICAL STUDIES

From the study of Bultmann, an important conclusion can be drawn for Catholic Biblical scholars and those who read them: *In the study of the Bible, particularly the New Testament, we may use to the full extent of their value the tools, such as the study of literary forms, which Bultmann and others like him have devised. However, we must be careful to exclude erroneous preconceptions.* In other words, we can follow his methods, but not his philosophy.

This holds true particularly concerning his teaching about Jesus Christ. We can accept all solid scholarship about the way in which the gospels were composed and written. However, we cannot be led to reject the miracles which Christ worked as a sign that He was sent by God just because some philosopher, without proof, declares that God cannot intervene in His creation. Nor can we accept the denial or watering down of the divinity of Jesus Christ merely because this same philosopher states that nothing can be divine.

The central mystery of Christianity consists in the belief that God became man, that "the Word was made flesh and dwelt among us" (John 1:14). "This is the victory that overcomes the world, our faith. Who is there that overcomes the world if not he who believes that Jesus is the Son of God?" (1 John 5:14)

As Jesus was walking one day in the porch of the temple, the Jews said to Him: "How long dost thou keep us in suspense? If thou art the Christ, tell us openly."

Jesus answered them, "I tell you and you do not believe. The works that I do in the name of the Father, these bear witness concerning me. But you do not believe because you are not of my sheep. My sheep hear my voice, and I know them and they follow me. And I give them everlasting life; and they shall never perish, neither shall anyone snatch them out of my hand. What my Father has given me is greater than all; and no one is able to snatch anything out of the hand of my Father. I and the Father are one" (John 10:22-30).

Discussion Points

1. How do the ideas of Catholics and rationalists differ with regard to: 1) the divinity of Christ; 2) the meaning, purpose and effect of His life among men?

2. What does Bultmann mean by "demythologizing" Scripture?

3. If we accept Bultmann's rejection of the supernatural, what is left of the content of the New Testament after it has been "demythologized"?

4. Explain the method of "form criticism."

5. Bultmann declared: "I believe in the event of Christ but not in the events of Christ." What did he mean?

6. Why are the historical events in the life of Christ of no importance to Bultmann? What is his view of salvation history?

7. What is meant by the *kerygma?* How does Bultmann's concept of the *kerygma* differ from that of traditional Christianity? Discuss this question thoroughly until it is clear to all that, according to Bultmann, man is saved only by faith in the gospel message, not by the objective truth of the message. Show how for him this faith is purely subjective, without any base in reason or in history.

8. Why is it said that Bultmann offers us "a total reinterpretation of Christianity according to a particular type of rationalistic philosophy"? How does this appear, for instance, in his explanation of sin? Explain how, according to him, belief in the death and resurrection of Jesus saves us from the "sinful seeking for security and certainty through the example of his "openness to the future."

9. What does Bultmann mean by "openess to the future"? Does this differ in substance from the "courageous despair" of Heidegger?

10. Bultmann has had immense influence upon modern Protestant and Catholic Biblical studies. Show the care that must be taken by the Biblical scholars and those who read them to exclude the erroneous preconceptions on which many of Bultmann's conclusions are based.

11. Bultmann rejects all the miracles of Christ because these would require the intervention of divine power in the world. Can a Christian follow him in this rejection? Why? In this connection, discuss the statement of Nicodemus: "Rabbi, we know that Thou hast come a teacher from God, for no one can work these signs that Thou workest unless God be with him" (John 3:2).

CHAPTER X

MAN'S ENCOUNTER WITH GOD BY FAITH

As we have seen, many liberal Protestants, under the guidance of such men as Harnack, Tillich and Bultmann, have discarded all, or practically all of traditional Christianity. They attempt to substitute for it a type of subjective, rationalistic Christianity which is rather a philosophy than a religion.

However, this movement has not gone unchallenged. The battle between liberal and orthodox Protestants has been fiercely fought for over one hundred years. And it has lost none of its vigor today. Recently in Germany, for instance, orthodox Protestants refused to attend a nationwide religious gathering unless the names of certain liberals were erased from the list of speakers.

KARL BARTH

One of the leading figures in this struggle within Protestantism has been Karl Barth (1886-1968). He was a pupil of Harnack in Berlin, and in his early days adopted the liberal ideas of his master. However, Barth's later experience as a Protestant minister soon revealed to him the poverty of this type of religion. This was brought out for him particularly by the blood and anguish of World War I. Barth's people were crying out to him for the bread of the Spirit and he had nothing to give them except a stone.

Hence, he began to look for the true meaning of life not in subjective philosophy, but in the word of God as revealed in the Holy Scriptures. Faith, he teaches, is necessary to accept this message of God. However, once it is accepted, it provides the key to man's ultimate worth and destiny. It opens to him the way to a life of courage and hope, a life dedicated to the love of God and of one's fellow man.

However, Barth was never able to shake off entirely the vestiges of subjectivism. Although he accepts the Bible as the word of God, his approach is still subjective. For him, man's certitude about religious truth comes from faith. But, as he explains it, this faith is a purely internal act, sufficient unto itself, without any need of rational foundation or evidence of credibility.

When God's word is presented to man, Barth declares, he has no right to investigate its claims to be the truth. His duty is simply and solely to believe.

INTERNAL LIGHT OR EXTERNAL WORD?

The distinction between subjective and objective religion is the focal point of some of the most important questions of the day. In fact, it is the whole thesis of this book that much of the present confusion and controversy in the Church is the result of failing to distinguish properly the relationship between God's objective revelation and the inner religious experience in the consciousness of man.

Does God reveal himself immediately and directly to the human mind and heart, or does He reveal himself mediately through the Bible and the teaching of the Church? This question has many aspects. Is religion purely internal and subjective, or is it also external and objective? Is God's revelation of himself to man independent of history, or has He revealed himself in the events of salvation history as described in the Bible?

We may also ask: What part does Christ play in God's self-revelation to man? What is the role of the Church with relation to the Gospel message?

Are we brought to accept the word of God by an "inner light," or by external signs, such as miracles? Is faith a matter of the mind or of the heart? By what steps is a man led to make the act of faith? What part does the grace of the Holy Spirit play in leading man to faith?

What does it mean to say that faith leads to a "personal encounter with Christ and with God"? Does this mean that there are no "truths of faith"? Was God's revelation of himself made once for all through Christ and the apostles, or does He continue to reveal himself as history goes on?

What is the difference between God's revelation of himself to man during his mortal life, and after death in the beatific vision?

In summary, how far does revelation consist in: 1) an act of God; 2) an event of history; 3) a type of knowledge; 4) an encounter?

No one can presume to give complete answers to all these questions. They involve what is probably the most difficult section of all theology. Not only that, but here we arrive at the heart of mystery: How can the infinite God, in His wisdom and mercy, find ways of communicating himself to His finite creatures, and of uniting them to himself in the love of friendship?

Although we cannot solve all these questions, let's try at least to throw some light upon them: 1) by explaining some incorrect solutions that have been advanced; 2) by showing the connection that must exist between God's external, objective revelation of himself through Jesus Christ and the interior act of faith by which man encounters God as revealed in His word, and enters into communion with Him.

SUBJECTIVE RELIGIOUS EXPERIENCE

Whenever there are several different aspects to a theological question, the danger arises that one side will be stressed and others disregarded. Today, some writers emphasize the internal, subjective character of religious experience to such an extent that they disregard or deny its external, objective foundation.

Actually, it is only since the time of Descartes and Kant, with their break between the mind of man and external reality, that the possibility of an objective revelation by God to man has been doubted or denied. Nevertheless, the seeds for this had already been sown in Protestantism by its rejection of the teaching authority of the Church and its insistence on private interpretation of the Bible.

With every man his own interpreter, different religious opinions sprang up on every side. In fact, it was Luther himself who declared that, even in his day, every milkmaid thought she could start her own religion.

Since one man's opinion had no more claim to be correct than another's, men tended to shy away from the intellectual search for truth and to put the emphasis on internal, affective religious experience. Religion became a matter of the heart rather than of the mind.

From this position, it required only a step to deny altogether the external, transcendent character of revelation and to turn it into something purely human, a form of religious sentiment. In Germany, for instance, Ritschl (1822-1889) reduced God, revelation, salvation and all other doctrines to an entirely immanent religious experience. Religion, for him, does not come from God; it is built up in the heart of man. There are no dogmas or creeds; faith is merely an affective disposition of the soul.

Much the same position was adopted by the French Protestant, Sabatier. He rejects any idea of a revealed positive truth. For him religious doctrines come and go. They can be altered or discarded. It doesn't matter, because the only important thing is the religious sentiment which they inspire.

MODERNISM

At the beginning of the twentieth century, a similar movement called *Modernism,* appeared among Catholics. It likewise rejected all unchanging religious truths, and made religion consist in an interior experience, an awareness of man's relationship to God. Two of its principal exponents were A. Loisy in France and George Tyrrell in England. Modernism was condemned by Pius X in 1907.

OTHER SUBJECTIVE CATHOLIC THEORIES

Without implying that they have any connection with Modernism, one can discern in some recent Catholic books a tendency to make man's knowledge of God immanent, immediate and direct. It must be admitted, however, that the authors' statements on this point are often vague and tentative.

As mentioned before, Leslie Dewart in his *Future of Belief* suggests that man is somehow aware of God as a *presence,* but not as a *being.* On the other hand, he admits that another person, looking at the same evidence, might interpret it as showing an *absence* of God. He certainly implies that since we now "have come of age," all the traditional ideas connected with an external, objective revelation must be revised. In fact, it is very difficult to conceive how his type of God could speak to man at all.

Michael Novak, in his *Belief and Unbelief,* seems to find God in his own consciousness, in the internal processes of his mind. He writes: "To believe in God is not to accept the conclusion of a deduction. It is to accept the evidence that one discovers in one's own knowing and doing, indicating the presence of a God who remains unseen and even unconceptualized. It is, above all, to enter into a conversation with that God, not through words so much as through the direction of one's intention" (p. 152).

Again he writes: "The step into God's presence is achieved in a fashion that can be described, but not accompanied by detailed instructions. One comes to trust one's own drive to understand. Then, quite simply, one begins to speak, even though God is hidden. If one's preceding reflections are correct, one stands already in His presence" (p. 156).

Brother Gabriel Moran's *Theology of Revelation* and *Catechesis of Revelation* have received wide acceptance in catechetical circles. In these books, man's "encounter with God" is the key idea to his theology and catechetics. However, in some passages he speaks of this encounter in such a way that it seems to imply some sort of immanent, immediate revelation of God to the individual.

PUBLIC REVELATION

"The individual is not normally the direct recipient of revelation," states the *Theological Dictionary* of Karl Rahner and H. Vorgrimler. This means that the good news of the Gospel, God's self-revelation of himself in salvation history, is made known to mankind not by private revelation, but in the public revelation made through Jesus Christ, preached by the apostles, recorded in the Bible, and interpreted by the Church.

PRIVATE REVELATION

God can, if He so wills, speak directly to individuals. However, the Church has always held that such private revelations are extraordinary. She does not presume to pass a final judgment affirming the truth of such private revelations. She will, at times, declare their human credibility, and state that nothing in them is contrary to the official public revelation.

ANY NEW REVELATION?

Was Christian revelation a once for all thing, or has

God continued to reveal himself through the ages? We must here make a distinction. The content of public revelation was completed with the death of the last apostle. No new truth can be added to it. However, the meaning of this revelation can be ever more deeply sounded. To put the matter simply: God speaks no new word to us beyond that which He spoke to us in His Son. But He continues to speak this same word to us through the centuries. We must receive this word by faith and ponder its meaning in our hearts.

NATURAL AND SUPERNATURAL

How does God reveal himself objectively to man? He does so in two ways: 1) in creation; 2) in His Son. The first of these we call *natural* revelation; the latter, *supernatural.*

We need not here delay on the concept of natural revelation. Let it suffice to say that through creation we can know the existence of God and something about His divine nature. That we can know the existence of God through creation was officially defined in Vatican Council I. That we can know something of His nature is clear from St. Paul: "Since the creation of the world his invisible attributes are clearly seen— his everlasting power also and divinity—being understood through the things that are made" (Rom. 1:20).

However, this natural revelation does not make known to us the intimate nature of God or His divine plan to bestow upon men the gift of supernatural life. This He has revealed through Jesus Christ, His incarnate Son, the Word made flesh.

ROLE OF THE CHURCH

Through the words and actions of Christ, we have the authentic communication of God's plan of salvation. This plan encompasses not only the Jews of

Christ's time, but all men, in every age. Since by the Father's will, Jesus was not to remain personally on earth, for the continuation and application of His work of redemption to all mankind, He established His Church. As the foundation stones of His Church, He chose twelve simple, unlearned men. He made Peter, a fisherman, their leader. To this unlikely group He gave the commission to go forth into the world to announce and to carry on the work of redemption.

The apostles occupy a unique place with respect to Christian revelation. Christ called them to be His companions, hearers of His word, witnesses of His actions. To them He made known all things that He had heard from His Father (John 15:15). The words He received from the Father He gave to them (John 17:8). As Christ was sent by the Father, so they were sent by Him. Whoever receives them, also receives Christ and the Father who sent Him.

After Pentecost, the apostles, enlightened by the Holy Spirit, went forth to proclaim the Gospel, the good news of salvation. Those who hear this apostolic preaching are called to respond by faith. "Go into the whole world and preach the Gospel to every creature. He who believes and is baptized shall be saved" (Mark 16:16).

Hence we do not enjoy the immediate, concrete experience of the person of Christ which the apostles possessed before the resurrection. What we receive is the apostolic testimony concerning Christ. This testimony is heard by the ear and assimilated by the mind. Christ occupies the central place in this teaching, not as directly and immediately known, but as the object of faith. In other words, we encounter Christ in the teaching of His Church.

FAITH AND ENCOUNTER

Some Protestants have rejected the idea of a deposit of revelation, of a body of truths received from Christ and the apostles, and proclaimed by the Church. They emphasize rather that revelation is an act, a divine intervention in history for man's salvation. Faith, they say, consists in man's acceptance of this act, his existential encounter with God through Jesus Christ.

However, this still leaves the question open as to how this encounter is effected. Is it purely subjective, an immanent, direct experience of God or of Christ? How do we reconcile the word "encounter" with the fact that the object of faith is not immediately and directly perceived? The answer to this important question is admirably expressed by René Latourelle in his *Theology and Revelation.*

"Catholic theology is the first to admit that revelation is an *activity,* an *event,* an *encounter,* which upsets the whole existence of man and calls him to a decision, to a commitment of his whole person; but Catholic theology adds, faithful always to the realism of the incarnation, that the encounter with Christ and His mystery is effected only through hearing the apostolic witness, handed down through the Church and consigned to Scripture. It is by adherence to the apostolic doctrine that we touch on God and His mysteries; it is through the fragility of conceptual and verbal signs that we have access to the very reality of Christ: not only through them alone, but with the aid and penetration of the light of faith. Adherence to the Kerygma, to the message, is a means of encounter and communion with the person" (p. 374).

THE INNER LIGHT

To present religion merely as a series of propositions, a set of questions and answers to be memorized, is to deprive the Christian message of its life and vibrancy. It is to miss its stirring call to commitment and to action, to the dedication of oneself completely to

God through Christ—heart and soul and mind and will.

On the other hand, we cannot represent man's contact with Christ and with God during His mortal life as though it were a direct and immediate knowledge. During life we walk in faith. We see as through a glass, darkly. Even in the mystic states of contemplation, man's knowledge of God retains this character of faith.

This faith is a gift of God. Man cannot arrive at it by his unaided powers. It is true that by reasoning man can arrive at the threshold of faith. He can recognize its credibility. But it is only by grace that he can be led across the threshold and actually make an act of supernatural faith.

Again and again, the Scriptures emphasize the need of this interior movement of the Holy Spirit, who by His grace moves men to the act of faith.

Jesus put it very simply when He said: "No one can come to me unless the Father who sent me draw him" (John 6:44). Again He declared: "No one can come to me unless he is enabled to do so by my Father" (John 6:66). St. John wrote: "It is the Spirit that bears witness that Christ is the truth" (1 John 5:6).

The Acts of the Apostles shows how this interior movement of the Spirit works in practice: "A certain woman named Lydia, a seller of purple from the city of Thyatira, who worshipped God, was listening; and the Lord touched her heart to give heed to what was being said by Paul" (Acts 16:14).

Theologians describe this interior activity of the Holy Spirit, drawing men to believe, as an interior instinct, an inclination, an attraction. They are careful to point out, however, that the interior experience of faith must always conform to the external word of God, as proposed by the Church.

The history of Christianity supplies abundant proof, even from the time of the apostles themselves, that a man can mistake the product of his own mind and imagination for divine revelation. The internal, subjective idea must be tested upon the anvil of God's word, proposed in the Scriptures and interpreted by the Church, to whom alone Christ promised the unerring guidance of the Holy Spirit until the end of time.

Discussion Points

1. What is meant by a purely subjective faith? Is it possible to discuss religion with a person—Catholic, Protestant, Jew, Mohammedan or Buddhist—who simply declares: "I believe what I believe because I believe it; there is no other reason"?

2. Does God reveal himself immediately and directly to the human mind and heart, or does He reveal himself in the Bible and the teaching of the Church?

3. Why does insistence on the internal, subjective aspect of faith tend to make religion a matter of the heart, rather than the mind? Show how this attitude normally leads to a rejection of all dogmas and creeds, of all objective and unchanging religious truths. Tell what you know about the Modernist movement among Catholics in the early part of the twentieth century.

4. Can we discern present day trends among Catholics to make man's knowledge of God immanent, immediate and direct?

5. What is private revelation? Does God ordinarily reveal himself immediately and directly to men?

6. Did God's public revelation of himself to man close at the death of the last apostle, or does it continue through the ages?

7. What is natural revelation? Why do subjective theologians tend to shy away from the fact that we can know God through creation?

8. Explain the role of the Church in safeguarding and interpreting divine revelation.

9. What is meant by saying that faith is "an encounter with Christ"? Do we encounter Christ immediately and directly or through the Church?

10. Explain the necessity of the grace of the Holy Spirit for making an act of supernatural faith.

11. Show the need of testing one's personal ideas of religion by comparing them with the word of God revealed in the Scriptures and interpreted by the Church.

CHAPTER XI

DOES LOVE NEED LAWS?

When two sets of husbands and wives get bored with each other, is it all right for them to swap partners for a while?

May housewives run a daytime house of prostitution to get those little "extras" which every woman wants, as long as no harm is done to husbands and children?

Is it just good clean fun for the college crowd to set up a pad where narcotics and free love are the central attraction?

Each of these situations, and many more like them, have recently been exposed to view in the newspapers and on TV. That's not particularly shocking, since experienced persons have always known that such things were going on. What is a matter of concern, however, is that such modes of conduct are beginning to receive widespread acceptance, and even to be defended as legitimate expressions of freedom among adults.

ANYTHING GOES

The moral attitude governing all this for many seems to be: "Anything goes! There is no such thing as moral right or wrong."

Others don't go quite that far. They qualify the statement a bit by saying: "Anything goes, as long as you don't harm someone else. Or if you do step on someone, it must be for a good reason."

The principle underlying such attitudes is this: No human actions are morally right or wrong in themselves. They become moral or immoral only according to the circumstances and purpose for which they are done. In other words, there is no intrinsic, or absolute morality.

This position is merely a logical application to human conduct of the subjective and relative philosophy accepted by so many persons today. If there is no unchanging truth, there can be no unchanging morality.

If there is no God who creates man with a determined human nature and directs him to an ultimate purpose according to a providential plan, there can be no talk of any absolute morality.

If man consists of nothing more than changing states of consciousness, without permanence or objective reality, all he can be expected to do is to live in the way that seems best to him from moment to moment. If he is selfish, he will adopt the attitude: "Eat, drink and be merry; for tomorrow we die!" If he is noble and unselfish, he will say: "Let me do a little bit for others in the brief moment that is mine." This unselfishness may bring personal peace and satisfaction. However, without God who calls man to eternal life, the end of either course is the same: the extinction of consciousness when death blows out the lamp of life.

SITUATION ETHICS

One of the most popular proponents of subjective and relative morality today is Dr. Joseph Fletcher. He calls his system "Situation Ethics." He has written a book with that title, now in paperback, with the subtitle, "The New Morality."

We can summarize the teachings of situation ethics under three headings: 1) the rejection of absolute moral laws; 2) the primacy of love; 3) the need for concern.

NO ABSOLUTE MORAL LAWS

We must not suppose that Fletcher rejects all moral principles whatsoever. He merely declares that no moral principle is absolute. According to him, all admit of exceptions in various circumstances. He may, for instance, agree that adultery is wrong in general, but maintain that it is lawful, and even virtuous, for a woman to commit adultery in order to provide for her children.

The core of situation ethics, as Fletcher describes it, is: "A healthy and primary awareness that circumstances alter cases, that is, that in actual problems of conscience the situational variables are to be weighed as heavily as the normative or general constants" (p. 29).

An analysis of situation ethics reveals that it is based on four assumptions. 1) Relativism, the view that there are no absolute and unchanging principles of truth or morality. 2) Subjectivism, which maintains that conscience does not judge according to an objective law, but makes up its own internal laws. 3) Personalism, which declares that the human person requires freedom from all externally imposed rules and laws. 4) pragmatism, which holds that all goodness and truth are measured only by practical results, by the benefits they produce.

Fletcher himself deduces some of the consequences of his approach. He proposes the question: Is it right to have premarital intercourse, to lie, to steal, to perform mercy killing, to cause an abortion, to defraud, to break contracts? He responds: "This kind of intrinsicalist morass must be left behind as irrelevant, incompetent and immaterial. The new morality, situation ethics, declares that anything and everything is right or wrong, according to the situation" (p. 124).

INTRINSIC RIGHT AND WRONG

In opposition to Fletcher, traditional Christian morality maintains that some actions are intrinsically right or wrong. That is, they are right or wrong of their very nature, apart from the circumstances or the purpose for which they are done.

There are, indeed, some actions that are by their nature morally indifferent. These have no intrinsic connection with the moral law. Eating, drinking, walking, talking, sleeping are examples of such indifferent actions. Of themselves, they are neither good nor bad. However, they can become good or bad according to the circumstances in which they are performed or the purpose for which they are done. Sleeping, for instance, is good if done in moderation to restore one's bodily power. However, it is morally wrong for a soldier on sentry duty deliberately to go to sleep, if this puts the lives of his companions in danger.

However, there are other human actions which have an intrinsic relation to the moral law. They are right or wrong of their very nature, apart from the circumstances or the purpose for which they are done.

We can discern such intrinsic morality in each of the four chief fields of human action:

1) *In man's actions with relation to God.* Man is a creature of God. Therefore, by his very nature he owes to God reverence, obedience and love. Hence such actions as blasphemy and hatred of God are intrinsically wrong. The love of God and obedience to His will are intrinsically right.

2) *With relation to man's use of material things.* God has given man these material things for his welfare and not his destruction. Hence the deliberate use of such things as narcotics, alcohol or poison in such a way as to destroy rather than benefit his body is intrinsically wrong.

3) *With relation to the use of his own bodily and mental powers.* Man is not master of himself; he is a creature of God. Hence it would be intrinsically wrong for a man deliberately to destroy his own use of reason or to cause his own death by deliberate suicide.

4) *With relation to his fellow men.* Man is by nature a social being. Hence those actions are intrinsically wrong which are essentially contrary to social living, such as wilful murder, injustice and hatred.

Because of their fundamental character, such intrinsically right and wrong actions constitute the chief subject matter of the natural law, the Ten Commandments, the revealed moral law of God, and the moral codes of all nations.

Actions that are intrinsically wrong continue to be so under all circumstances, and no matter for what purpose they are done. For instance, wilful murder is the directly intended killing of an innocent person. This is always wrong, under all circumstances, and for any purpose, however good.

Some persons seem to think that the purpose is the sole determinant of the morality of an act. However, to say this is to declare that the end justifies the means, that we are allowed to do evil in order to produce good.

THE PRIMACY OF LOVE

After repeating many times that anything and everything is lawful to man in certain situations, Fletcher states one principle that he considers absolute, which must always be followed in making decisions. This is, he says, the law of love. For him, the only intrinsic good, the only unchanging value, the only law to which there is no exception is that of love.

His doctrine is simply summed up in the words: "No law or principle or value is good as such—not life or truth or chastity or property or marriage or anything but love. Only one thing is intrinsically good, namely, love; nothing else at all" (p. 60).

LOVE AND INTELLIGENCE

A Christian can go a long way with Fletcher in his emphasis on the importance of love. The love of God and the love of one's fellow man for the sake of God is the supreme determinant of all morality. Moreover, it is love alone that gives human action merit before God. St. Paul was very clear about this. Actions, even apparently the most noble, are worthless and unprofitable unless they are motivated by love.

There is a difference, however, between true Christian love and that described by Fletcher. True Christian love recognizes the duty to obey God's commandments and to fulfill His will. "If you love me, keep my commandments."

On the other hand, Fletcher's idea of love leaves no room for such an objective norm. It recognizes no need of conforming to God's law. Its decisions are purely subjective and relative.

In Fletcher's presentation, love is a vague, unpredictable, undefinable thing. His idea of love involves even contradictory notions. On the one hand, he declares that love is the only regulatory principle of Christian ethics and human behavior. On the other hand, he says that love is not something objectively real, or predetermined or capable of being defined or even described. Love is something that appears in an action, not something that can be planned or intended before the action. Love supplants all other laws. Murder, adultery, incest—any kind of action—can under certain circumstances, he says, be justified by love.

What this basically amounts to is that love is divorced from intelligence. The will is free from regulation by the mind.

He even applies this doctrine to God. He quotes with approval an old axiom of the nominalists: "God does not command things because He knows beforehand that they are good; rather anything becomes good because God commands it." This removes intelligence from the divine governing of the world. It implies that everything that is now morally evil could have been commanded by God, if He so willed, and everything that is now morally good could have been prohibited.

Such a doctrine, if led to its logical conclusion, would ultimately destroy all difference between good and evil. The truth is that God is not only infinite love, but He is also infinite intelligence. He was not obliged to create man. However, once man is created, God must, by the infinite holiness of His own divine nature, direct him according to his nature to the purpose for which he was made.

LOVE AND LAW

In the complexities of human life, love needs the direction of law. Otherwise it can become destructive. The woman who abandons her husband and children to run off with another man says that she is motivated by love. So does the mother who renders her children unfit for life by spoiling them, giving in to their every whim. So does the burglar who steals to buy diamonds for his girl friend. Each of these claim that they are acting out of love. But it is a blind, unregulated, destructive love.

Love needs the guidance of law. Suppose there were no traffic lights or stop signs. Everybody is simply told to drive in such a way that they show their love for their neighbor. Soon traffic in our large cities would be so hopelessly snarled that no one could move in any direction.

It is true that men in authority at times multiply laws needlessly. Sometimes, too, they overemphasize the legal structure, without reference to the true purpose of law and without regard for the primacy of love. This is the legalism which Fletcher rightly condemns. However, we cannot go to the opposite extreme and declare that we need no law except love. Human society would fall into chaos.

JUSTICE AND CHARITY

The gaps in Fletcher's system appear all the more clearly in his treatment of justice. "Love and justice are the same," he states, "for justice is love distributed, nothing more."

Here Fletcher has to retreat from a previously held position. He has insisted many times that love is not to be limited or directed by reason. It is a law unto itself, overriding all other laws.

Now when the practical difficulty arises of distributing love to many persons in the complex situations of human life, he suddenly acknowledges that prudence and intelligence are required. "Prudence," he says, "careful calculation gives love the carefulness it needs; with proper care, love does more than take justice into account, it becomes justice" (p. 88). In fact, he is led to the admission: "When we see love in this way, we are forced to pull back from the sentimental and irrational idea that love is not intellectual."

In his treatment of justice and charity, Fletcher makes a blunder which reveals that he really knows very little about Catholic moral teaching. He declares that Catholic moralists teach that the virtues of justice and charity are distinct, and that justice is obligatory but charity is optional. "All Catholic moralists," he writes, "separate them (that is, justice and charity), making love a 'supernatural' virtue and justice a 'natural' virtue, holding that we *must* be just in our actions but only *may* be loving" (p. 93). He expresses surprise that the usually logical Catholic moralists hold such an absurd position.

The position is indeed absurd; but the truth is, Catholics don't hold it! In Christian life, both charity and justice are supernatural virtues, and there is nothing optional about either of them. We are obliged both to love our fellow men for the sake of God and to render them that which is their due. In other words, justice is the application of charity in the special field of human rights.

It is not enough to be loving toward our neighbor in a vague and general way. We must also respect his rights to his life, to his human dignity, to his good name, to his property.

Again Fletcher falls into vagueness when he tries to describe the practical working out of love and justice. Justice, he declares, is nothing but love working out its problems with many neighbors. But, we may ask, what standard does love use in working out these problems? He answers that we must consider what will give "the greatest amount of neighbor welfare for the largest number of neighbors" (p. 95).

Here we are back to the old norm of John Stuart Mill and other relative moralists. They say that morality must be determined by the principle: "We must do the greatest good for the greatest number."

It is amazing that Fletcher cannot see the evil consequences which will follow from this principle if it is applied without regard to the rights of individuals. This principle would justify the oppression of any individual or minority group for the sake of the majority. On this basis, for instance, Hitler could justify the murder of six million Jews because he considered that this would promote the welfare of sixty million Germans. In the same way, this principle would justify a doctor in killing the deformed baby at birth if he thought that this would be better for the family. It would also permit the assassination of a political or religious leader if one considered this to be good for the country.

Fletcher and the situationists fail to recognize that true love can flourish only in an ordered society in which men have respect for the rights of their fellow men. These rights are established by the law of God and protected by human law.

To put it very simply, love should be the motive of

all men's actions. However the way this love works out in the complexities of human life must be determined by law, and ultimately by the law of God directing man according to his nature to the purpose for which he was created.

Discussion Points

1. Is the state of morality today as bad as it is pictured in the newspapers and on TV? Are young people less moral than their parents, or are they only less inhibited?

2. Which factors would you consider most important in the apparent breakdown of public morality: 1) the lack of clear moral standards; 2) abandonment of parental responsibility; 3) bad example; 4) irreligious education; 5) the impact of movies and TV?

3. Why is the denial of absolute moral principles the logical consequence of subjectivism and relativism in philosophy and religion?

4. Is it possible to construct a coherent and effective system of morals without reference to God?

5. What is meant by "situation ethics"? Why does Fletcher consider this a middle ground below legalism and lawlessness? What is his primary principle?

6. Point out the assumptions which underlie his rejection of absolute morality?

7. Upon what basis does traditional Christian morality maintain that some human actions are intrinsically right or wrong? Show how we can discern intrinsic right and wrong in the four chief fields of human action.

8. What's wrong with this statement: "Anything is all right as long as it is done from a motive of love"?

9.   Are things good only because God commands them, or does He command them because they are good? Are things evil only because God prohibits them, or does He prohibit them because they are evil?

10.   Why does love need the guidance of law? What would happen in a society where all laws were abolished?

11.   What's wrong with Fletcher's principle that morality must be determined by what will do the greatest good for the greatest number? What would be the consequences if this principle were applied without regard to the rights of individuals and of minorities?

12.   Discuss the statement: "Love can flourish only in an ordered society in which men have respect for the rights of their fellow men. These rights are established by the law of God and protected by human law."

13.   What would happen if morality were made dependent upon the subjective judgment of each individual in each particular situation?

CHAPTER XII

PUTTING THE PIECES TOGETHER

At this point, it is time to try to put together the pieces of knowledge we have gained in previous chapters and to try to organize them, as best we can, into a complete picture.

It is clear that much of the confusion in the Church today results from the clash of two different mentalities, or ways of looking at things. One is objective, the other subjective.

The objective viewpoint begins with the world outside of man. It recognizes man as a part of this world and subject to its laws. He has been endowed with faculties of knowledge precisely in order to come into contact with this external world and to use it for his own physical, mental and moral development. Man has been made to know this real world of which he is a part. He does not immediately and directly know his own act of knowing. He knows himself reflexly in the act by which he knows other things. The objective approach places its emphasis on the object, the *datum* the content of knowledge rather than on the very act of knowing.

The subjective viewpoint takes as its starting point the consciousness of man. It looks out at the world through human eyes. It is concerned with the way things seem to man, with their value for him. It centers its attention on man's thoughts and emotions, his search for his own identity, for the meaning of life as seen from within. It is concerned with man's freedom to think and to choose, to be his own master, free from external coercion.

When explained in such general terms, there need be no contradiction between the objective and subjective way of looking at things. Each gives us a partial but correct view. They must be blended together in order to get the total picture. There really is an external world which does not depend upon the consciousness of man for its existence. There is also an internal world of human consciousness which is composed of man's thoughts and feelings, his ideas and emotions.

Each of these approaches is right in the positive values it asserts. Each falls into error when it disregards or denies the truth of the other side. The objective approach, when pushed to its extreme, can produce a world that is *depersonalized*—legalistic, authoritarian, preferring things to people, devoid of warmth and love, indifferent to human hunger, poverty and pain.

IDEALISM

On the other hand, the subjective way of looking at things becomes false and erroneous when it places a gap between the mind of man and the real world. It then gives rise to the false philosophy of idealism, which declares that the object of man's knowledge is not the real world, but his own thoughts.

In the period since Descartes, who first set up this gap between the mind of man and the world of reality, there have been developed many types of idealistic theory.

Some go all the way and declare that there is no real world outside the mind of man at all. Thought is the only reality; matter is merely a delusion.

Others admit the existence of an external world, but deny that man can know anything about it. His own faculties of knowledge distort the picture, so that he does not know reality, but merely the appearances of things.

Still another theory accepts the validity of sense knowledge, but declares that man cannot know any truth which transcends the senses. Hence, according to this theory, all ideas of spiritual things, such as God, the soul of man, moral right or wrong, are merely projections of man's own mind, without objective existence or truth. Of course, all the more forcefully, this theory rejects any idea of the supernatural.

All the above systems are aberrations of the subjective approach. They mistakenly insist too much on the subjective side of knowledge, and deny its objective value. Volumes would be required to trace the historical origin and development of each of these idealistic systems. Even more volumes would be required to examine them critically and to show their incompatibility with the common sense of mankind and with Christian revelation. It will be enough for us here to establish some basic points.

IMPOSSIBLE TO LIVE BY

The idealistic position that man can have no true knowledge of the world outside his mind is impossible for mankind to accept and to live by. Of course, it is possible for a person by adopting some such devious method as Descartes or Kant, to work himself into such a speculative position. But to try to follow this in real life would lead to mental and physical destruction. A college professor, for instance, may teach his class that man cannot be sure of anything outside his mind. After class, however, he goes home, kisses his wife, plays with his children and cuts his lawn. If he were consistent with his teaching, he couldn't know for sure that he has a wife or children or lawn.

The very examination of man's body reveals that he is constructed to know the world outside himself. His eyes look outward, not inward. His ears are evidently made to catch the vibrations of sound. His nose has external apertures to admit odors from without. His mouth opens to receive food. His arms and hands are made to reach for, to feel and to handle objects. His legs and feet enable him to move from one place to another.

No intelligent person can look at himself or any other human being and reasonably deny that man is made to know a world outside himself.

SUBJECTIVISM AND RELATIVISM

Many of those who claim to speak for the "contemporary mind" base their stand on one of the false forms of idealism described above. They can't find a way to cross the gap that, in their opinion, separates the mind of man from the world outside him. Hence they declare that man can never arrive at absolute truth, that is, truth about things as they are in themselves. They maintain that he can attain only relative truth, that is, about things as they appear to him.

The consequences of this position are many, especially in the field of philosophy and religion. Starting from such a viewpoint, for instance, man could never reason to the existence of God, the Creator of the universe, since he could not be certain that any such universe really exists. Again, he could not be certain of the truth of any objective revelation by God, such as that contained in the Bible and taught by the Church, since he could not be sure that any God exists outside his own mind. Whatever religion such a man possessed would have to be purely personal and subjective, with no possible criterion for judging its objective truth.

BASIC NATURAL TRUTHS

The Christian religion is not tied down to any particular philosophical system. However, Christianity presupposes certain basic natural truths and must reject any philosophy which denies them. Such truths are, for example: 1) that the mind of man can attain to objective truth; 2) that there is a God, personal, intelligent and distinct from the world; 3) that man is spiritual as well as material, endowed with intelligence and free will, capable of knowing and observing the objective moral law, and capable of receiving from God the gift of supernatural life.

Christian revelation is incompatible with the rejection of any of these basic truths. It cannot, therefore, be reconciled with subjectivism and relativism, which deny that man can know objective truth. Nor can it accept the extreme existentialism of such men as Heidegger, Sartre and Camus, which looks upon man as merely a succession of changing conscious states, without continuity and without any permanent spiritual principle.

There is, however, no sound reason why the subjective approach to things through the avenue of human consciousness need be pushed to such extremes. There is no valid reason why, because man can know himself, he cannot know also the world outside himself. The gap between the mind of man and the external world does not really exist at all. It has been set up by the specious, but erroneous arguments of certain subjective philosophers.

We must, then, take a central position between an impersonal objectivism which disregards the unique position of the person and the dynamic character of human life and, on the other hand, the extreme subjectivism which would imprison man's knowledge within his own mind. In other words, we must put at the service of Christian revelation a complete philosophy which does justice to the plentitude of being and at the same time recognizes the unique place of the human person in God's creation.

Let's see how this synthesis can be applied to some of the important questions which confront the Church today. Perhaps by taking a position above and beyond the "old" theology and the "new," by accepting what is good in each of them and correcting what is defective, we may catch a glimpse of some new solutions to old problems.

REJECTION OF THE SUPERNATURAL

Probably the most serious problem confronting the Church today is the rejection by some who call themselves Christians of the whole supernatural character of the Christian religion. We have always had our professed atheists and agnostics. This is a fact which saddens, but does not surprise or shock us. However, it is an all together different matter for a professed Christian, particularly a minister of religion, to present Christianity in such a way that it is transformed from a revealed religion to a naturalistic philosophy.

The difficulty is compounded by the fact that naturalistic ideas are often presented in terms which have always carried a traditional Christian meaning, such as salvation, sin, redemption, commitment to Christ, etc. This rejection of the supernatural extends even to the concept of God himself. We have seen how Paul Tillich and others who follow him, such as Leslie Dewart, have emptied the concept of God of all its supernatural content. God is no longer Father, Protector, Friend. He no longer watches over and cares for His people. He does not call them to share His own divine life and happiness. He is reduced to an indefinable "ground of being," or "open background of consciousness," or some other vague phrase.

We have also seen how Rudolf Bultmann empties the concept of Christ of all supernatural content, as completely as Tillich empties the concept of God. For Bultmann, Jesus Christ who lived on earth was not "the Word made flesh." He was not divine; nor did He possess any divine powers. He gave to the world no divine revelation; neither His words nor deeds possessed any supernatural value.

Nevertheless, according to Bultmann, it is by faith in Christ, by acceptance of the *Kerygma,* the apostolic message about him, that the world is saved. However, according to Bultmann, this message is wrapped in myths and symbols. It must be "demythologized" in order to arrive at its real meaning. When Bultmann finishes his process of demythologizing, there is nothing supernatural left in the Gospel. Although Christian and Biblical terms are retained, the underlying message is nothing more than the agnostic existential philosophy of Martin Heidegger, with its "lonely decision," its "courageous despair," its "openness" to a future unknown even to God.

NEW FORMS BUT OLD TRUTHS

The fact that naturalistic philosophy is now being presented in Christian terms places a heavy burden both on the average reader and on the theologians. It boils down to this: We must be ready to accept everything of genuine value in the "new theology"; but we must not be deceived into accepting a naturalistic substitute for the essentially supernatural Christian religion. Nor can we allow to go unchallenged the introduction into Catholic theology of ideas that are incompatible with Christian revelation.

The religious confusion and turmoil which surround us today are not a direct result of Vatican II. The Council documents themselves are an admirable blending of the old and the new, of personalist values with traditional Catholic teaching. They present the unchanging Christian truth in a dynamic, vibrant way. They draw from the riches of Christian revelation new applications to problems of today's world.

However, not all theologians, Biblical scholars and popular writers have been as prudent. As a result of the new climate of theological freedom, Catholics have suddenly become aware of the extensive world of Protestant scholarship, of which hitherto few Catholics outside the European universities had any knowledge. The trouble is that some Catholics have uncritically accepted not only what was genuinely valuable in such scholarship, but have also taken over the philosophy of such men as Harnack, Tillich and Bultmann, apparently without realizing that this involves a denial of the supernatural and a rejection of a great part of the content of Christian revelation.

We must, indeed, speak to contemporary man in language he can understand. However, the message we must announce to him is the good news of man's call to supernatural life through Jesus Christ.

THE SACRED AND THE SECULAR

Another key idea in the religious picture today is the relationship of religion to the secular world. Is the principal purpose of the Christian religion merely to help build a better world in which man can live during his mortal life? Or is it to lead men to supernatural life which will continue after death?

This question is absolutely fundamental to religion. The answer a man gives to it will shape his entire attitude toward life and all that it contains. Christian revelation teaches unequivocally that each man is called to everlasting life, to a conscious personal immortality which consists in the possession of God through knowledge and love. For the Christian, then, life is not meaningless and absurd. It is something God-given, God-guided, with a purpose worthy of God. Believing that Jesus Christ is truly "the Word made flesh, that He died and rose again from the dead, Christians accept with the fullness of faith the tremendous promise of eternal life.

On the other hand, the anguish spoken of so frequently by agnostic and atheistic philosophers and theologians, comes not only from the sufferings of life, but from the fact that these must be endured without hope. Their concern to build a better world on earth is born of the despairing thought that this short mortal life is all that any man will ever have.

Vatican Council II emphasized the point that Christians must work earnestly for a better world, for the cure of the grievous ills that beset mankind today, for the building up of a more just and brotherly city in this world.

However, the Christian approaches this task of building a better world from a far different viewpoint from that of the agnostic or atheist. It is important to emphasize this, since it is precisely in this connection that some of our eager Catholic laymen, priests and nuns have lost their perspective and, as a result, suffered a "crisis of identity."

The Christian works to remake human society precisely in order that God's plan "to re-establish all things in Christ," may be fulfilled. The mission of the Church and of each Christian, whether priest, religious or layman, is to work for the accomplishment of this divine purpose, to bring every nation and each individual soul into God's eternal kingdom.

This means that we must strive to remake the world so that it will provide each man with the best possible chance to receive and develop the gift of supernatural life.

It is our task, with God's help, to enable every man to live not in poverty, hunger and ignorance, not in hatred and fear, but in dignity and freedom, in brotherhood and love, sharing God's creation here on earth, waiting for the blessed hope and coming of His Son.

The parish priest who refuses to administer the sacraments in order to engage in social action, or the Sister who no longer wishes to teach religion to children so that she may go out "into the market place" has perhaps confused the means with the end. As

Christians, we cannot make the temporal welfare of men the final goal of our work for them. Christ worked His miracles of healing in order that men might believe and, believing, have life in His name. So too, all our efforts for the temporal welfare of mankind must have the ultimate purpose of bringing men to God, in whom they will find eternal life.

This does not mean that we will work with less dedication or devotion for the relief of the miseries of mankind and for the establishment of justice and charity on earth. But it will mean that we do it for a supernatural motive. The recognition that our ultimate goal is to bring men to eternal life will also make us realize that the final success of our work will depend not only on our own efforts, but also on the help of God. It will bring home to us, too, the need for prayer as well as action, since God's help is promised only to those who ask for it.

Discussion Points

1.   Explain the difference between the objective and subjective approach to the nature of man and his problems. Show how each of these viewpoints must be blended into a total view of truth.

2.   To what excesses does the objective viewpoint lead when it loses sight of personal values?

3.   Show how the subjective approach becomes the false philosophy of subjectivism when it places a gap between the mind of man and the real world. Review briefly the development of the philosophy of subjectivism.

4.   What's wrong with the statement: "Man can only be certain of what he can observe with his senses; he can never be sure that rational principles have validity outside his mind"?

5.   What are the consequences for religion of accepting a philosophy of subjectivism and relativism? What happens to the existence of God, objective revelation, the Bible, the Church?

6.   Why is Christianity incompatible with any philosophy which denies: 1) the ability of the human mind to attain objective truth; 2) the existence of a conscious, intelligent personal God; 3) the spiritual nature of the soul, or vital principle in man?

7.   Discuss the statement: We must place at the service of Christian revelation a complete philosophy which does justice to the plentitude of being and at the same time recognizes the unique place of the human person in God's creation."

8.   Describe the attempts of Tillich and Bultmann to transform Christianity from a revealed religion into a naturalistic philosophy. How can we separate what is genuinely valuable in the scholarship of such men from their erroneous philosophy?

9.   In what spirit does a Christian work to make a better world here on earth? How do his efforts differ from those who believe that this mortal life is all that any man will ever have?

Chapter XIII

EVOLUTION AND CHRISTIAN THOUGHT

When man looks at the universe, of which physically he is such an infinitesimal part, he is confronted with mystery. Over his head on a clear night, pinpoints of light glow in the darkness. These tiny, distant flickers of light, he knows, are huge burning suns, rushing through space at incredible speed in orbits of unimaginable size.

Where did they come from? What ignited their fires? What force set them speeding on their swift way? They must have had a beginning. For not even the greatest suns can burn forever.

The earth on which man stands has its own wonders and gives rise to its own questions. Here and there are hints of its origin and its long history. For instance, the rocks at the bottom of a deep canyon reveal that they were formed some two billion years ago. Bubbling patches of hot mud and the white plumes of geysers remind us that the crust of the earth is just a shell, beneath which banked fires still burn. In a few secret places, we find footprints or fossil remains of strange animals long vanished in the past.

Most mysterious of all is man himself. Part of him is kin to the earth and the matter of which it is made. From it, he takes the food which he transforms into himself, and the breath without which he could not live. Earth's elements are blended in his body, and into them it dissolves when he comes to die.

And yet there is a part of man which gives evidence that it is in no way kin to matter. This is the part of him that shows itself as mind and will, intelligence and love. A material container can hold just so much, and no more. However, the mind of man never reaches a point in which it is filled, in which it can contain no more. The more a man knows, the more he can know, and the more he seeks to know.

The mind of man roams through the depths of space and measures the distances between the stars. He can take into himself and make his own the perfections of all other things. That is why Aristotle exclaimed in wonder: "The soul is, as it were, all things!"

No one has even come close to explaining in terms of matter the power of human thought, with its grasp of the abstract and universal aspects of things, its perception of immaterial ideas such as truth and justice, its ability to judge and reason, and its consciousness, its power to reflect upon itself and its own acts.

The same is true of human love, especially the conscious, mutual unselfish love between two persons. The mind revolts against identifying the warm, living, tender, spiritual bond of love with the cold, dead, inanimate world of matter. Love is a union of spirit. It recognizes in the other values that are spiritual and permanent. That is why a man says to his beloved: "I will love you forever!" That is why, too, he is ready, if need be, to sacrifice his life for his loved one.

Whence came this mysterious being which we call man, who shows himself now as matter, now as spirit; bound to earth, yet reaching for the sky; made of clay, yet in the image of God?

Many modern minds, both Christian and non-Christian, try to find an answer in what they call "evolution."

Many speak of evolution as though it were a single thing. However, as we will see, this is an extremely complex idea which has been presented in many different forms. It has important ramifications in science, philosophy and religion.

TYPES OF EVOLUTIONARY THEORY

There are many different types of evolutionary theory. They differ profoundly in their explanations of the extent, the form, the cause and the purpose of the evolutionary process.

The various theories concerning the origin of the universe depend, of course, to a great extent upon the author's interpretation of the nature of the universe as we now find it.

Materialists maintain that the only reality is matter, which has been arranged in various ways by the process of evolution to constitute the different kinds of things we have today. *Idealists,* on the other hand, hold that the only reality is thought, the stuff of which our consciousness is made. Matter for them is merely an illusion. This thought, or mind, the idealists declare, is developing toward ever more perfect forms. Most idealistic theories end in some form of pantheism, the doctrine which identifies God with the world.

Spinoza advanced the idea that reality has two sides: one material, the other spiritual. If we look at things from the outside, they appear as matter. If looked at from the inside, they take the form of consciousness, or thought. Both, he says, are developing together toward more perfect forms.

Pluralist theories assert that there is more than one essential level of being in the world. They hold that the characteristics of life and mind are so different from matter that they cannot be explained as merely different arrangements of matter. Therefore, they say, there are at least three irreducibly different levels of being: matter, life and mind.

THE EXTENT OF EVOLUTION

Unrestricted, or total evolutionary theories extend the process to the whole of the universe. Everything that exists now, they say, has come from some cosmic dust, or primitive forerunner of matter.

Restricted theories of evolution begin the process at

some particular point. Many, for instance, refuse to admit the generation of living things from inorganic matter. All the evidence, they declare, shows that material compounds tend to break up and become more simple, rather than to become more complex. Hence, they say, it is a blind act of faith, totally contrary to all scientific evidence, to say that matter, by developing ever more complex forms, emerged into life.

THE PROCESS

Again there is disagreement with regard to the form of the evolutionary process. Some hold that development advanced in a smooth orderly fashion, with the higher coming from the lower by gradual transition. Others say that this is contrary to all evidence, and that the only way evolution can be explained is by a series of leaps, or jumps, in which the higher emerged from the lower without transitional forms. When restricted to living things, these jumps are called "mutations."

THE CAUSE OF EVOLUTION

Christianity, and indeed many other religions, declare that, in the light both of reason and revelation, God, the ultimate reason for the existence of things, is *transcendent*. That is, He is in no way part of the world, identical with the world, or evolving to perfection with the world. By His infinite power, not only has He brought all things into existence, but He is the reason for their complexity and diversity.

As long as God is recognized as transcendent, it makes no particular difference to the Christian whether the way the world came to be what it is today is, or is not, the result of a total or partial evolutionary process. He is perfectly willing to accept whatever evidence is presented for or against any particular type of evolutionary theory. Of course, Christian revelation is incompatible with any system which explicitly or implicitly denies that there is in man a spiritual principle which is capable of receiving the gift of supernatural life which God gave to man through Jesus Christ.

Many modern writers, because of their agnostic or atheistic philosophy, refuse to admit the transcendence of God. They attempt to explain the course of evolution as a result of an immanent force, or forces, working within the evolutionary process itself.

Most of these authors are reluctant to come to grips with such problems as: 1) Where did the original stuff of which the world is made come from? 2) What started and maintains the process of evolution? 3) Why has the world been evolving onward and upward toward newer and more complex, instead of backward and downward toward more simple forms?

Writers who try to answer such questions in terms of a purely immanent cause for evolution usually end up in some form of pantheism. They declare that God himself is being formed or developed or perfected through the process of evolution. In their books we read such phrases as "a *nisus,* or tendency, toward deity"; or "God as emergent in the process of evolution." In other words, they turn the Christian idea completely around. Instead of God being the Creator of the world, God is created by the world. Moreover, since man is at present the highest point of evolutionary advance, for them man is God. This will serve to explain many statements which fall harshly on Christian ears.

THE PURPOSE OF EVOLUTION

Those who accept an unrestricted theory of evolution must face up to the question: Is there a purpose, an end or goal toward which this whole process is tending? Has the onward rush of the universe a meaning, or is it all irrational and meaningless?

The answer which one gives to this question will tie in closely with his interpretation of the cause of evolution. *Mechanistic* theories reject any design, purpose or intelligence in the cause of the process of evolution. They attribute development to purely mechanical causes, acting without purpose or design, in an entirely fortuitous way. To put it simply, they say that everything happened *by chance*. The elements of the primordial stuff of the universe began to act and react and eventually, without any direction whatsoever, arrived at the various complex and stable combinations which we see around us today. This, in their interpretation, is the way a piece of lead or zinc came into existence. It is also, they say, the complete explanation of the origin of man, with his power to think and to love.

Teleological, or purposive, theories contend that evolution without purpose or direction is absurd and impossible. They hold that the progressive advance of evolution can only be explained as a result of the gradual working out of a purpose, or design. But is this purpose *conscious* or *unconscious?* In the transcendental theories mentioned above, this purpose is the conscious intention of the supreme intelligence, who is God. In the pantheistic, immanent theories of many modern philosophies, this purpose is understood as a blind, unconscious tendency.

This brief outline of evolutionary theories has been presented in order to bring out the fact that evolution is indeed a very complex idea. It is not enough to say: "The world as we know it today is the result of evolution." Evolution is not a cause, but a process. Even if we accept an unrestricted theory of evolution, we must still ask the questions: Where did the "stuff" of which the world is made come from? What was it like? What started it evolving? Has this evolution any direction or purpose? How explain the coming of life? Of mind? Is God the cause and guide of the evolutionary process, or is He himself evolving with the world?

Books could be written on the various answers that have been given to these questions. Hence it has been impossible here to do more than outline the various types of evolutionary theory.

TEILHARD DE CHARDIN

However, there is one writer who has exercised such an influence upon liberal Catholic thought, particularly since Vatican II, that we must single him out for particular attention. This writer is Teilhard de Chardin, S.J.

His undoubtedly brilliant, imaginative and creative mind has elaborated an evolutionary view of the universe which blends together science, faith, philosophy, mysticism and Christian theology. He envisions the course of evolution as one grand sweeping panorama in which everything, under the hand of God, moves in a single, unbroken line from the simplest beginnings to the absorption of mankind into God. In this way, he gives a mystical sense to evolution. Christianity is integrated with "cosmogenesis," that is, with the evolutionary development of the world. For him the Christ of the gospels must be assimilated to "the cosmic Christ," who is the origin and the end of evolution. Christ is presented not as the Redeemer but as the "evolutor" of the world.

Chardin's ideas are so revolutionary, and his language so liable to different interpretations that a lively controversy has sprung up about him.

One group sees in him a man of prophetic vision, whose ideas are capable of reconciling Christianity with modern science, and making it acceptable to "the contemporary mind."

Those on the other side declare that his work falls

into the class of "theology-fiction." It is, they say, the product of a lyrical imagination, with no solid foundation in science, reason or revelation. In their opinion, it distorts the whole meaning of Christianity, confusing the material and the spiritual, the natural and the supernatural, in a system which, in spite of the undoubted good faith of its author, is at least suggestive of pantheism.

It is evidently impossible here to attempt to settle the differences between those who favor and those who oppose the ideas of Chardin. For our purpose it will suffice to point out some of the areas of conflict, so that anyone who reads or discusses Chardin may be awake to the problems.

MATTER AND SPIRIT

Does Chardin confuse the material with the spiritual and hence arrive at a false idea of the origin, nature and destiny of man? One of the major problems for anyone who accepts an unrestricted evolutionary theory is to explain the origin of mind. For a Christian evolutionist, who believes that man is called to, and capable of receiving supernatural life, the problem is all the more difficult.

Chardin tries to find a solution in the dual aspect theory of Spinoza, previously described, which declares that all reality is both matter and spirit. Looked at from the outside, it is matter; from the inside, it is spirit.

However, opponents say, this doctrine is purely arbitrary, advanced without a shadow of proof, and in direct opposition to experience. There is nothing in the physical world to substantiate the claim that it is endowed with a concomitant psychical attribute. The qualities of physical and psychical are clearly and sharply divided. One is material, quantitive, extended; the other immaterial, qualititive, inextended. Thus they have contradictory properties, and it is impossible to identify them as two aspects or attributes of one single underlying reality.

The sole reason, it is said, for advancing such an idea is the wish to render more plausible the evolution of mind from matter. But this is the very point under discussion. Hence to identify mind and matter without proof is to beg the question from the very start. Indeed, it is a tacit confession that it is impossible to evolve mind as we know it from matter as we know it. Hence, they assert, we must reject such an interpretation as the foundation of a sober and reasonable interpretation of reality.

ORIGIN OF THE SOUL

Chardin also runs into difficulty with regard to the origin of the soul, or the spiritual principle in man. His system is hostile to the traditional doctrine of the immediate and direct creation of each human soul by God. For this, to him, would demand the intervention of God in the evolutionary process. If his idea of the psychical nature of all reality is rejected as being without proof, he is left with the dilemma: a) either the spiritual principle in man arose from matter; or b) it is not spiritual at all.

Chardin has much the same problem with regard to the question of immortality. According to his doctrine, consciousness arises when matter becomes more and more complex, as in the human brain. But logically, then, consciousness should disappear when death dissolves the matter of the brain into its elements.

THE SUPERNATURAL

What of the supernatural character of Christian revelation? In fact, how does any concept of divine revelation fit into a system of evolution which is presented as allowing no intervention from without? This concept of the evolution of supernatural life, which is a sharing in God's life by those who are baptized, would seem to be the greatest difficulty of all for Chardin's system.

If his approach is accepted, the meaning of almost every Christian idea would have to be changed. In the New Testament, man is portrayed as freely accepting or freely rejecting the call to enter God's kingdom: "Repent, for the kingdom of God is at hand." But what is the place of free will when the course of evolution is portrayed as necessarily sweeping onward and upward?

Moreover, the whole concept of moral evil would have to be revised. For Teilhard, sin is not moral but metaphysical. "It is," to quote him, "a turn of bad luck," in the progress of the universe. Original sin is explained as the fact that all creation, physical and biological, is impregnated with evil.

In this way, as Chardin himself points out, the central notions of traditional Christianity—creation, spirit, evil, God, sin, the cross, resurrection, judgment, charity—will have to be transposed into "dimensions of cosmogenesis."

But, it may be asked, does such a transposition of Christian ideas conform to the divine revelation which God gave us in the Scriptures and through His Church? Or, as Jacques Maritain would have it, is this a Christianity turned upside down, a distortion of the gospel, a mad hope for the advent of a "better" Christianity celebrating the glories of the cosmos?

Chardin envisions the final state of humanity as one in which individual men merge into a "superconsciousness." He doesn't explain very clearly what he means by this. But his words convey the idea that there will be more than a merely moral union, such as is expressed by the phrase that two persons become "one heart and one soul." He seems to be describing more than that—some sort of state in which all humanity has only one thought and one act of will. When mankind reaches this state, he says, it will be united with Christ, who is the Omega Point toward which the evolution of the whole universe, matter and spirit, has been tending. All creation, thus united with Christ, will be absorbed in God, until finally "God is all in all."

Many claim to see in such a description at least overtones of pantheism. They point to statements of Chardin in which he says that God is "the soul of the World"; that there is a "fusion of God and the World"; a "mutual completion of the World and God." Even though Chardin did not intend his words to be taken in a pantheistic sense, there is danger that those who read him will interpret his statements to mean that the being of the world will eventually be absorbed and identified with the Being of God.

GETTING BACK TO PRINCIPLES

When we consider the relationship of Christian thought to evolutionary theory, we can state the following principles:

1) The Christian faith neither demands nor denies an evolutionary interpretation of the universe. It is quite content to await the evidence.

2) The acceptance of an evolutionary theory of the universe does not, as some have mistakenly supposed, dispense from the necessity of God as the ultimate reason for the existence and development of the universe.

The world exists, and is composed of diverse and complex things. That is a fact which no sane man can deny. But to assert that this complexity and diversity of things came into being merely by chance, by the movement of some cosmic dust or primitive forerunner of matter, without purpose or design is simply absurd. For something even as complicated as an automobile to come into existence simply by chance, without a design, would be utterly improbable. But to assert that the myriads of things that make up our world, many of them supremely more complex than an automobile, arose merely by chance is totally unthinkable. Hence purely mechanistic theories of evolution have been almost completely abandoned.

There remain then only two alternatives. Either we accept God or we explain evolution as the result of a blind, unconscious purpose, a nisus or tendency, which is moving the universe onward and upward toward ever more complex and perfect forms.

However, when we examine critically this concept of a blind, unconscious purpose or tendency toward perfection, we find that it is equally impossible to accept. A blind force, acting without a predetermined goal, would have no reason to go in one direction than another. Hence, the invoking of such blind forces, or tendencies, is completely incapable of explaining why the universe is tending toward more complex and perfect forms, rather than toward those that are simpler and less perfect. The whole idea of a blind force moving without conscious direction toward ever increasing perfection is a contradiction. Consequently, an intelligent man must acknowledge that the world can only have come into existence and developed to its present complexity and diversity as the result of a Power directed toward a conscious, intelligent purpose. This Power we commonly call God.

3) The picture of God which is given to us by our intelligence is completed and perfected by the revelation which God has given to us of His plan to bring all men to share His divine life through Jesus Christ, His incarnate Son. The story of this revelation is given

to us in the Bible and interpreted for us by the Church, under the guidance of the Holy Spirit.

In his faith, a Christian finds assurance that his life is not meaningless and absurd. His life is not merely "a fleeting spark between two eternal darknesses." The world on which he lives is not merely "a burned out cinder, revolving around the sun with its cargo of human fools."

The Christian walks through life knowing that he is not at the mercy of a blind, unreasoning fate. He is in the hands of a loving Father, whose providence leads all things, though at times and in ways hard for man to understand, to His glory and the welfare of those who love and serve Him. *For those who love God all things work together unto good.*

For those who do not know God, the grave is the end of all human hope and love; and for them the final end of the universe can only be the revolving of burned out stars in the blackness of unending space. That is why we read on the tombs of ancient pagan Rome the message of despair: *Farewell forever!* In the same way, the modern atheist calls us to his doctrine of "courageous despair."

THE CHRISTIAN ANSWER

Here is the glory and strength and comfort of the Christian faith: that God himself gives us the answer to the riddle of life, to the mystery of the universe, through Jesus Christ, His Son.

Why did Christ come into the world? He came to bring us the gift of divine life: "I have come so that they may have life and have it to the full" (John 10:10).

Only Jesus Christ, the Word of God made flesh, could speak that tremendous sentence which banishes forever man's uncertainty, darkness and despair: "I am the resurrection and the life. If anyone believes in me, even though he dies he will live, and whoever lives and believes in me will never die" (John 11:25).

Discussion Points

1. What is man's normal reaction when confronted with the mystery of the universe? Is man only an infinitesimal dot in the vastness of space? Or is he greater than the whole physical universe?

2. What did Aristotle mean when he said: "The soul is, as it were, all things!"

3. Distinguish between the scientific theory of evolution and evolutionism.

4. What type of evolutionary theory will be held by a materialist? An idealist? A follower of Spinoza? A pluralist?

5. What is meant by an unrestricted theory of evolution? Is such an extension of the evolutionary process based on scientific evidence?

6. Explain the theory of Teilhard de Chardin. How is he regarded by modern Catholic writers? Discuss Chardin's ideas with regard to: 1) the nature of reality; 2) the origin of the human soul; 3) the supernatural character of the Christian life; 4) the final destiny of man.

7. Do you think that Chardin's ideas can be reconciled with Christian revelation? Or do you agree with Maritain that his doctrine is theology-fiction, a distortion of Christianity?

8. Can the complexity and diversity of the world be explained as the product of chance, operating without direction?

9. Bring out the inherent contradiction in the idea of a blind force moving without conscious direction toward ever-increasing perfection.

10. Show how any evolutionary theory must be completed and perfected by God's revelation of the meaning and destiny of human life given to us through Jesus Christ.

11. Contrast the hope of the Christian, trusting in the providence of God with the "courageous despair" of the atheist and agnostic.

CHAPTER XIV

CONTROVERSY ABOUT THE DUTCH CATECHISM

The controversy concerning the *Dutch Catechism* highlights many of the ideas concerning religion which we have discussed. For this reason, even though at present parts of it are being rewritten, we will try to analyze carefully the manner in which it presents the Catholic religion. For the underlying philosophy which it adopts reflects the religious approach of many moderns, both in and outside the Catholic Church. Moreover, the book applies this new approach to specific doctrines of faith and morals. For this reason, a discussion of the controversial first edition will continue to have value, even though the book is later rewritten or superseded.

When we speak of the *Dutch Catechism,* we are referring to the first American edition of the book entitled *A New Catechism,* with the subtitle *Catholic Faith for Adults.* It was published in 1967 by Herder and Herder, N. Y.

IS IT APPROVED?

It is not often that a book can raise a storm over the simple question of whether it has, or has not, received an *imprimatur*. However, the *Dutch Catechism* has managed to do this in a big way. (The *imprimatur* is the official permission from a bishop required by Canon Law before the publication of a Catholic book on religion.)

This permission was given for the original Dutch edition by Cardinal Alfrink of Utrecht. However, after the book appeared, protests were made to Rome about its contents. One group of Dutch Catholic laymen wrote: "The book presents many ideas that either blatantly contradict the faith or explain various truths of faith so ambiguously that every reader can decide for himself whether they are orthodox or not." The protestors then singled out seven particular points which they claimed are contrary to Catholic faith.

Because of the uproar, a commission was set up in Rome to examine the book. The result of this examination, as given in newspaper accounts, is not entirely clear. According to one version, the commission stated that the book contained no formal heresy, but that certain sections should be rewritten. One of the men asked to help in this rewriting, Father Visser, a Dutch theologian residing in Rome, is a little more definite. He is quoted as saying that the original version contained "errors" which should be corrected.

This work of rewriting, it seems, has not gone too smoothly. The representative of the Higher Catechetical Institute at Nijmegen, Holland, which produced the first edition, is said to have withdrawn from the work in protest over the changes that were demanded.

In the meantime, a translation into English was in preparation. At first, Bishop Robert Joyce, of Burlington, Vt., gave his *imprimatur*. However, he withdrew this when he learned that the English version would be published without waiting for the revision commanded by the commission. This withdrawal came too late for the British edition, which was already in print. The publishers decided to go ahead with the American edition, even without the required *imprimatur,* merely citing that given for the original Dutch edition.

Cardinal Alfrink is quoted in *Osservatore Romano,* November 2, 1967 as stating that he "deplored the English version of the catechism which was carried out without his responsibility and before modifications could be made in the text."

In the same way, Cardinal Frings of Germany has

strongly protested the German translation of the book, which likewise was published without waiting for the required changes.

In a joint statement, the bishops of the United States declared that they cannot recommend this first edition as a text for the teaching of religion.

WHAT'S ALL THE FUSS ABOUT?

The fact is, that the *Dutch Catechism* can be read from two different points of view.

According to the first, the catechism gives us a needed up-dating of the expression of the Catholic religion. This is the view expressed by Father Gerard Sloyan: "Beautifully written and well translated, this volume is in every way a suitable guide to the meaning of Christian life in today's world." Father Bernard Cooke, S.J., takes the same stand: "An excellent presentation of the more up-to-date understanding of Catholic teaching."

The blurb on the cover of the American edition proclaims that the catechism presents "an adult religion" for those who have "come of age." It emphasizes that the book is not for "the child who leads a submissive, compliant existence, sheltered against danger." It is for the mature, responsible, self-reliant Christian, who is not satisfied with traditional though unsatisfactory solutions to controversial problems, who has both his faith and his doubts. To this man invitation is given to be a responsible, participating believer, who has "set aside the things of childhood."

OPPONENTS

Those who hold the opposite point of view claim that the catechism presents not merely a change in the expression of Catholic beliefs, but a change in the very substance of such beliefs. Or at least, they say, its presentation is so ambiguous that the meaning of important truths, such as the spirituality and immortality of the human soul and the existence of heaven and hell, is left in doubt.

Opponents point out that the very terms used by defenders of the catechism to describe it have been borrowed from liberal Protestants. Such terms are: "adult religion," "Christianity come of age," "faith which sets aside the things of childhood." These are the very phrases used by Tillich, Bultmann and others who consider the traditional Christian message as too childish and naive for contemporary man, and wish to substitute for it a rationalistic humanism derived from such men as Harnack and Heidegger.

The accusation is also made that an imprudent excess of the ecumenical spirit has led the authors of the catechism to disregard, explain away or water down Catholic doctrines, such as the teaching authority of the Church, the importance of tradition, the existence of purgatory and the intercession of the saints.

WHAT PHILOSOPHY BEHIND IT?

The *Dutch Catechism* is certainly existential. There can be no doubt about that. However, the major question is: What type of existential philosophy is expressed or implied in its pages? Is it content with affirming personalist values, such as the freedom and dignity of man and liberty of conscience against external coercion? Or does it go beyond this, and express or imply a subjectivism according to which all religious truth is relative, changing from age to age?

The catechism evidently accepts to some extent the demythologizing of Scripture, emphasized by Bultmann and other liberal Protestants. But how far does it wish to go? What are we to think, for instance, of the miracles of the Old Testament and New? Do any of the accounts of such miraculous events contain historical truth, or are they merely projections of faith, set down at a later date? Did God actually give the Ten Commandments to Moses? Was Christ born of a Virgin Mother? What of the bodily assumption of Mary into heaven? Did any of these events really happen? Or are they merely symbolic statements of some more general beliefs?

What of morality? Are there objective moral laws, either known by reason or revealed by God, to which man is obliged to conform? Are there any human actions which are intrinsically wrong, so that they are forbidden under all circumstances, and no matter for what purpose they are done? Or is morality merely relative, changing even its principles from age to age, and subordinating these principles to the circumstances of particular cases? For instance, is Christian marriage, when all the requisites for validity have been observed, truly indissoluble? What if such a marriage breaks up without hope of reunion? May the parties enter another marriage while the first partner remains alive? If they do, and live as man and wife with the second partner, are they guilty of adultery? If they continue to live in this manner, may they receive the sacraments?

What is the relationship of personal conscience to objective moral law? Is conscience obliged to conform its decisions to the law? Or is conscience personal and subjective, with each man making his decisions as they seem best to him?

It is very difficult, if not impossible, to find answers in the catechism to many of these important questions regarding faith and morals. Not only are the problems themselves difficult, but the language is at times so ambiguous that the reader cannot make out clearly what the catechism is trying to say. We will point out examples as we go along. Opponents of the catechism suspect this ambiguity is not unintentional, but is used as a means of opening the door to excessively liberal opinions without openly stating them.

IS IT A CATECHISM?

Probably a good deal of antagonism could have been avoided if the book had not been called a "catechism." Ordinarily a catechism, even for adults, is thought of as a book of basic religious instruction. It is expected, therefore, that it will confine itself to safe and sane doctrine on which there is general agreement, and that it will avoid controversy and the projection of personal opinion.

However, the *Dutch Catechism* is not that kind of book at all! It is a presentation of Catholic doctrine from a particular philosophical and theological viewpoint. This combines traditional Catholic teaching with elements of existential philosophy. To this it adds the conclusions of certain modern Biblical scholars concerning literary forms and the demythologizing of the Bible. As a background it accepts a theory of unrestricted evolution.

This is set forth with an ecumenical preoccupation which seeks to remove wherever possible any expression of doctrine which might prove an obstacle to Christian unity. There is, besides, a great concern to present Christianity in such a way that it will appeal to the "contemporary mind," which by definition is hostile to the idea of absolute truth, and is forever questioning, searching, doubting.

All this constitutes a rather assorted kettle of fish. The contents certainly deserve to be sorted and identified. However, the *Dutch Catechism* does none of this. It takes its own approach for granted, as though it were beyond question. New ideas are presented as established truths. There is little or no attempt to line up theological opinions concerning particular problems and to weigh the arguments for and against them. Theological positions that have been accepted by the Church for more than a thousand years are dismissed with some such phrase as: "We don't speak that way any more."

This precise point is taken up by Professor Frederick Sontag, a Protestant professor of philosophy, in his commentary on the defense of the *Dutch Catechism* by Dr. Schoonenberg in *Herder Correspondence,* March 1967. He writes: "As Dr. Schoonenberg presents it, there is no question but that the *Dutch Catechism* is based on an elaborate set of philosophical principles. . . .

"Every philosophical theory, it would seem to me, needs to label itself as such, to recognize its constant need for defense and clarification and, most of all, for consideration of its strengths and its weaknesses as against other philosophical principles which might be used. . . . Does Dr. Schoonenberg really recognize and acknowledge systematically the highly controversial nature of his philosophical assumptions? If he simply assumes them as dogmatically true, then we are all in trouble."

PHILOSOPHY OF THE DUTCH CATECHISM?

What is this particular philosophy underlying the *Dutch Catechism?* This is not easy to identify because, as Dr. Sontag points out, the authors do not state and clarify the principles behind the positions they adopt on many important questions. They merely take these principles for granted and proceed as though there could be no doubt about them.

The whole question boils down to this: Does the *Dutch Catechism* contain a legitimate up-dating of the Catholic faith? Does it merely get rid of old outmoded language and ideas? Does it present Catholic doctrine in such a way that it appeals to "contemporary man" and makes easier the path to Christian unity? Or, as its opponents claim, is it so tainted with subjectivism and relativism that it changes not only the expression, but the essential content of the Christian faith as it has come to us from Christ and the apostles?

THE VIRGIN BIRTH

The question whether the *Dutch Catechism* changes merely the expression or the essential content of Christian faith comes into focus rather sharply with reference to the virgin birth of Christ.

Few doctrines seem to be more explicitly stated in the Gospels, more often mentioned by the Fathers of the Church, more constantly taught by theologians, and more tenaciously held by the universal Church through the ages than the doctrine that Christ was born of a virgin mother.

What does the *Dutch Catechism* say about his? First of all, it points out that there are a number of figures in the Old Testament, such as Isaac, Jacob, Samson and Samuel, whose birth was an answer to prayer. Then it goes on to say that the birth of Jesus was the answer to the prayer of a whole people and the promise of a whole history. "He was born wholly of grace, wholly of promise—'conceived of the Holy Spirit.' He was *the* gift of God to mankind.

"This the evangelists Matthew and Luke expressed when they proclaimed that Jesus' birth was not due to the will of a man. They proclaimed that this birth does not depend on what men can do of themselves—infinitely less so than in other human births. That is the deepest meaning of the article of faith, 'born of the Virgin Mary'" (p. 74).

Admittedly, these statements can be read in a sense which accords with traditional belief in Mary's virginity. But is this the sense intended by the catechism? A number of commentators read in these lines a denial, or at least a doubt about the virgin birth of Jesus Christ.

If it were only the opponents of the catechism who read this interpretation into it, we might be inclined to attribute this to prejudice. However, Dr. Piet Schoonenberg, S.J., professor of dogmatic theology in the city of Nijmegen, where the *Dutch Catechism* was published, clearly states: "The new catechism leaves the virgin birth an open question" (*Herder Correspondence*, May 1967, p. 159). He is certainly in a position to know the mind of those who composed the catechism.

There is no need here to go into an extended discussion of the virgin birth of Christ. The theological reasons are overwhelmingly in favor of the belief that Mary was a virgin before, during and after the birth of Christ. This is so clear that one wonders why any Catholic would doubt it. We begin to look for some preconceptions in the authors' minds hostile to the idea that Jesus did not have an earthly father.

The first reason why the authors of the catechism might be opposed to this idea is that it would require a miracle. This they don't like.

In a number of passages, they make clear that they wish to exclude, as far as possible, all divine intervention into creation other than by the normal working out of the physical laws of nature (cf. 107). This attitude, again, is probably the result of their acceptance of an unrestricted theory of evolution. The ordinary person would say: "If we believe that the Son of God became man, why should we boggle at the idea that He could be born without a human father? Scientists have already caused the birth of a live baby rabbit without a male parent, simply by stimulating the ovum of the female rabbit. Why could not the overshadowing power of the Holy Spirit do this in a woman?" However, the evolutionists, among whom are the authors of the *Dutch Catechism,* want no "intervention from without" in the evolutionary process.

There is a second reason why the authors of the *Dutch Catechism* look unfavorably on the doctrine of the virgin birth. Dr. Schoonenberg expresses it in his discussion of this question. He says: "At any rate, there is today a new reverence for earthly life, for marriage and for sexuality" (ibid., p. 158). The emphasis on Mary's virginity is seen as casting a shadow on the dignity of sexual union in marriage. Hence reasons are sought for interpreting the virgin birth as "a poetical expression of the unique divine sonship of Jesus."

We are, however, in trouble if we begin to twist Scripture and traditional Christian doctrines to meet our own philosophical preconceptions. In this way, we can read any meaning we want into Scripture. This is precisely the approach that has led Bultmann and other liberal Protestant scholars to "demythologize" the Scriptures to such an extent that there is nothing left of the supernatural content of the Gospels. In its place, as we have seen, such men have substituted a rationalistic humanism disguised in Christian terms.

It is also disturbing that the composers of the *Dutch Catechism* do not admit that they consider the virgin birth an open question. At first reading, the passages which refer to it seem to affirm the traditional doctrine. Only a careful analysis reveals that the authors may be attributing merely a symbolic meaning, rather than factual reality to the doctrine.

INTERCESSION OF THE SAINTS

The question then arises: Are there other passages in which the authors follow the same ambiguous procedure? What, for instance, does the catechism teach about the intercession of the saints, a belief that has been held in the Church from the first ages, and which has been defined by the Council of Trent?

On this point, the *Dutch Catechism* contains the following rather curious passages:

"The martyrs were envied and revered. They were not considered as figures of the past, but as living in paradise, wherever this was thought to be. Christians ask the martyrs to intercede with God for them. Thus the honor paid to the saints grew out of faith in regeneration" (p. 214).

With regard to prayer to Mary, we are told: "We can address her with confidence, if this helps us to see Jesus with new eyes and reach Him more easily" (p. 212).

Nowhere is it explicitly stated that Mary and the saints actually intercede for us with God. In fact, the explanation of immortality given by the catechism makes it difficult to understand how there can be any saints now in heaven to pray for us. We will take up this point in the next chapter.

Discussion Points

1. Why should we discuss the first edition of the *Dutch Catechism* when it is in the process of being rewritten?

2. Review the controversy over the *imprimatur* for the book. Do you think the publishers in the U.S. and Germany were justified in putting out translations before the required corrections were made? Have the bishops a special duty of watching over what is presented as "catechism"?

3. Describe the viewpoint of the defenders and of the opponents of the *Dutch Catechism*. What is the essential issue involved? Mention some of the specific issues raised by the attitude of the catechism toward the demythologizing of Scripture, the nature of the moral law, and the relationship of conscience to law.

4. Analyze the manner in which the *Dutch Catechism* combines elements of traditional Catholic teaching, existential philosophy, the conclusions of certain modern Biblical scholars, the ecumenical approach, and the attempt to appeal to the "contemporary mind."

5. Why is it necessary to identify the attitudes which underlie the position of the catechism with regard to specific doctrines of faith and morals?

6. Discuss the catechism's treatment of the virgin birth of Christ. How strong are the theological arguments behind this traditional doctrine? Why, then, would any Catholic deny or cast doubt upon it?

7. Bring out the danger of interpreting the Bible according to philosophical preconceptions.

8. What can you make out of the statements of the catechism regarding the intercession of Mary and the saints?

CHAPTER XV

THE DUTCH CATECHISM ON THE NATURE AND DESTINY OF MAN

The *Dutch Catechism* adopts without discussion a theory of unrestricted evolution, including the body and the consciousness of man. It clearly and definitely states: "The life in my body comes from the beasts" (p. 10).

How consciousness, with its power of intelligence, its perception of abstract and spiritual ideas, its freedom of decision, and its ability to reflect on its own acts, can arise from matter no one has yet come close to explaining. Consequently, the catechism finds the going a bit sticky here. However, it carries bravely, if vaguely on:

"It was once usual to say that God created the world and preserves it in being, but creates each soul directly each time. But this manner of speaking failed to do justice to two things, one, that creation itself is a reality which strives upward, and two, that body and soul are not to be divided.

"Hence it seems better to express the same truth in another way by saying that God's creative power causes reality to be and to grow at each moment. The beginning of a new human life is a sacred moment in which this creative power is particularly evident. After all, my parents could not have wanted 'me.' At best, they wanted 'a boy' or 'a girl.' Only God wanted 'me.' An 'I' which could say 'You' to God, have a direct and personal relationship with Him, is called into being through human heredity, and hence by the hand of God" (p. 382).

This passage evidently says that God does not create each human soul immediately and directly, that the human parents generate the whole man. According to the catechism, God's special part consists in the fact that he foresees and wishes to enter into personal relationship with each person.

The question then arises how the generative faculties of the parents, which are material, can produce the soul, or consciousness, of man, which gives every evidence of being immaterial.

THE NATURE OF MAN

Of course, the basic problem here is the distinction between matter and spirit. This question is absolutely fundamental in understanding the nature of man. Is there anything in man—call it *soul* or *spirit* or *life* or *consciousness* or *personality* or whatever you will — which is more than matter, which cannot be explained in terms of matter, which possesses operations irreducible to matter?

Classic Christian philosophy and theology declare that the vital principle, or soul, in man is spiritual. That is, it belongs to an order of being superior to matter. Its higher operations—intelligence and love—can in no way be explained as operations of matter. Precisely because of his spiritual nature, man is the image of God, and is capable of receiving supernatural life, which is a sharing in the life of God.

The question of the distinction between spirit and matter goes even deeper than the problem of the nature of man. It is absolutely fundamental to the whole concept of religion, because it also concerns the nature of God. God is a spirit and cannot in any way be identified with matter. If this is done, His transcendence is destroyed and we arrive at some form of pantheism. Since the authors of the *Dutch Catechism* find difficulty in accepting the existence of spirit apart from matter, it would be interesting to hear their explanation of the nature of God as He is in himself. Nowhere do they give such a description, as they are only interested in God as He relates to man.

As we mentioned before, various theories have been advanced in the history of human thought to explain the relationship between matter and spirit. 1) According to one view, all reality is spiritual and matter is merely an illusion. This position has been held by many idealists and by certain oriental religions. 2) According to others, the only reality is matter and spirit is an illusion. This is the philosophy of Communism and of materialism in general. 3) According to a theory developed by Spinoza and put forward recently by Teilhard de Chardin as the basis of his evolutionism, matter and spirit are two aspects of the same reality. Besides the fact that it is adduced without evidence, this theory flounders when it comes to God. Is God both material and spiritual? Or is God the spiritual side of the material world, a sort of all-pervading Mind? Because of this difficulty, in the past this theory has always led its followers to pantheism.

THREE ORDERS OF BEING

Traditional Christian philosophy and theology acknowledge three orders of being: 1) Purely spiritual, without any mixture of matter, e.g., God and the angels. 2) Purely material, without any mixture of the spiritual, for instance iron and stone. 3) Partly spiritual and partly material, that is, man. In this view, the soul and body of man are joined in substantial unity. Together they form one person. However, the soul of man is spiritual and capable of the spiritual actions of intelligence and will. Hence the soul does not cease to exist when the body dies. It enters a new and purely spiritual form of existence, until by the power of God it is reunited to the body.

The *Dutch Catechism* will have nothing of this. It rejects the idea of a soul, or a permanent spiritual principle in man. He is thought of as "an embodied consciousness," that is, a body in which by some mysterious process, there occurs a succession of continually changing conscious states.

However, with this view of man, the *Dutch Catechism* is hard put to explain: 1) The elevation of man to supernatural life, which consists in a sharing in God's own life. How can a purely material being share the life of One who is purely spiritual? 2) Personal immortality after death. If there is no distinction between body and spirit, if man's consciousness is totally dependent upon matter, when the body is dissolved at death, how can any element of consciousness remain? And if it does not, what becomes of Christ's promise of eternal life to those who believe in Him?

IMMORTALITY

Here the *Dutch Catechism* is in a bind. It is trying to combine with Christianity a type of existential philosophy which is really incompatible with Christianity, since it denies the existence of any permanent spiritual element in man. Let's look at some of the statements of the catechism in this regard:

> "The fibers of our being are so much part of the universe that we cannot think or make a decision without the processes at work in our brain cells, without the matter of this world" (p. 6).

This might be interpreted in the sense that only during life is man dependent upon matter for the processes of thought. However, the catechism makes clear that this is not its meaning:

> "Death is radical. It is not that just the arms, legs, trunk and head die. The whole earthly man dies. Here the deniers of immortality are right. Death is the end of the whole man as we have known him" (p. 470).

Does that mean that nothing of man remains, that the dead person has utterly disappeared, that nothing of consciousness survives? This should be the logical conclusion of a philosophy which rejects any permanent spiritual principle in man. If his consciousness is completely dependent upon his body for existence, when the body is dissolved by death, that should be the end of him.

However, this conclusion is so abhorent to Christian belief, and so evidently contrary to the promise of Christ, that no one who is truly a Christian can accept it.

Faced with this dilemma, the authors of the *Dutch Catechism* first present the idea that a person can live on after death through his influence on others (p. 471). This is certainly true; but it adds nothing to the viewpoint even of a pagan.

However, they go on to say that faith in the resurrection of Jesus and in His teaching about the resurrection of the dead makes us confident that we too are ultimately destined for eternal life.

According to the catechism, when and how this resurrection will take place is something we cannot know. The Bible, it declares, gives us no clear doctrine on the state of man immediately after death. The authors of the catechism reject as "unbiblical" the idea that man can continue to exist until the resurrection as a disembodied spirit. They say in this connection:

"The reason is that the Bible itself never thinks of the soul as entirely divested of all corporality. And modern thought lies in the same direction. What we are is so strongly linked up with our bodies that we cannot think of ourselves as an isolated 'I' disconnected from our body" (p. 473).

The latter statement, that we cannot think of ourselves as existing apart from our body is purely gratuitous. Christians, almost without exception, have always believed that each individual man will continue in a state of conscious immortality after the dissolution of his body.

What of the statement that the Bible never thinks of the soul as divested of all corporality?

It is true that the Jews of the Old Testament did not have a clear idea of man as a single being composed of matter and spirit, body and soul. This idea became possible only after the introduction of Greek philosophy with its distinction between potency and act. Nor did the ancient Hebrews have a clear idea of immortality, since this demands recognition of a permanent spiritual principle in man.

Most of the Old Testament simply portrays man as going down after death to *Sheol,* the abode of the dead. This is called "the nether world" in the translation used in the liturgy. For the Jews, this was a sort of shadowland, of which little was known, since no one had ever returned from there to describe it.

It was not a place of punishment. The idea of the punishment of the wicked after death appears in Jewish thought only toward the close of the Old Testament. The place of this punishment is called *Gehenna,* a term used several times by Christ (Matt. 5:22, 18:9).

Nevertheless, the Book of Wisdom, one of the last parts of the Old Testament to be written, makes the distinction between body and spirit and clearly teaches the immortality of the human spirit.

> "But the souls of the just are in the hands of God, and no torment shall touch them. They seemed, in view of the foolish to be dead; and their passing away was judged an affliction and their going forth from us, utter destruction. But they are in peace. For if before men, indeed, they be punished, yet is their hope of immortality; chastised a little, they shall be greatly blessed because God tried them and found them worthy of himself" (3:1).

The doctrine of the resurrection from the dead was bitterly disputed among the Jews before and during the life of Christ. When asked about this, Jesus simply answered: "As to the resurrection of the dead, have you not read what was spoken to you by God, saying, *I am the God of Abraham, and the God of Isaac, and the God of Jacob? He is not the God of the dead, but of the living*" (Matt. 22:31).

THE NEW TESTAMENT

The New Testament does not engage in a philosophical discussion of the make-up of man. It is concerned with religion, not philosophy. However, in many passages it speaks of man's spirit as the seat of supernatural life, the object of supernatural salvation.

1) It distinguishes between body and spirit: "Do not be afraid of those who kill the body but cannot kill the soul. But rather be afraid of him who is able to destroy both soul and body in hell" (Matt. 10:39).

2) The spirit is the principle of life which departs at death: "But Jesus again cried out with a loud voice, and gave up his spirit" (Matt. 27:50). "Father, into thy hands I commend my spirit" (Luke 24:46).

3) The spirit is distinguished from the body and the flesh: "Holy in body and in spirit" (1 Cor. 7:34). "Let us cleanse ourselves from all defilement of the flesh and of the spirit" (2 Cor. 7:1).

4) One who is baptized already possesses in himself the beginning of eternal life. He is "alive to God in Christ Jesus" (Rom. 6:11).

5) This life consists in knowing God in a special way: "This is everlasting life, that they may know thee, the only true God and him whom thou hast sent, Jesus Christ" (John 17:3).

6) The food of this life is the body and blood of Christ: "He who eats my flesh and drinks my blood

has life everlasting and I will raise him up on the last day" (John 6:55).

7) The task of the Christian is to develop this seed of eternal life within himself: "If by the spirit you put to death the deeds of the flesh, you will live" (Rom. 8:13).

8) One who possesses this life will never completely die: "I am the resurrection and the life; he who believes in me, even if he die, shall live; and whoever lives and believes in me, shall never die" (John 11:25).

NOT DEATH, BUT LIFE

The *Dutch Catechism* declares that at death the whole man dies. Such a position is demanded by the particular type of existential philosophy its authors have adopted. In favor of this view they mistakenly claim the authority of the Bible. Actually, such a view is incompatible with Christian teaching on immortality. Doubtless, then, this is one of the sections under revision.

If, as the catechism says, the whole man dies, what has become of the supernatural life received in baptism? The man is gone. His body soon dissolves into dust. Nor can it be asserted by the authors of the catechism that man's consciousness remains. For, according to their philosophy, consciousness is nothing more than a succession of psychic states, without any permanent principle. It is completely dependent upon the body and is extinguished with the dissolution of the body.

This is a conclusion which Heidegger, Sartre, Camus and others of their type are prepared to accept. It is the basis of their philosophy of "courageous despair." But it is completely unacceptable to a Christian. The message that breathes through every page of the New Testament is one not of death, but of eternal life in God through Jesus Christ.

The philosophy which the authors of the *Dutch Catechism* have adopted has led them into a dilemma from which they cannot logically escape. For them man's consciousness is so bound up with his material body that it cannot exist without it. For the "I" to exist after death, according to them, man must have some kind of body. So they advance the idea that man begins to get a new body at death. They say: "Existence after death is already something like the resurrection of the new body" (p. 474). However, they insist that this new body will not result from "reconstituting our earthly body" (p. 479). But this brings up the difficulty: If man's consciousness is so tied to his earthly body that it cannot exist without it, how can this consciousness be transferred to a new body? In other words, why is there not a new and entirely different man? In that case we would not have personal immortality at all. We would have merely the creation of new individuals.

As for this "new body," the catechism doesn't seem to be able to make up its mind whether it is received: 1) at the moment of death, 2) by a continuing process, 3) at the end of the world. Texts can be cited for all three positions (p. 473-479).

The idea of the resurrection as a gradual and continuing process is particularly difficult to understand. Yet there are a number of passages in the catechism which suggest this. Of the dead, it says: "They are about to rise. They are beginning to live with God" (p. 474). Speaking of the continuing influence of the dead here on earth, the catechism declares: "Some great saints and good men are more powerfully present than others. Does this perhaps indicate that they are already further on the way of resurrection?" (p. 476) Of this passage, we can only ask in utter bafflement: What can it possibly mean to say that someone is "further on the way of resurrection?"

The final destiny of man receives the same ambiguous treatment. Hell is presented as a state of "eternal sin." "The state of cold obstinacy has become eternal. . . . To be lost means to be entirely closed in on oneself, without contact with others or with God" (p. 480).

But what does this mean if man is nothing but a body in which there are succeeding states of consciousness? After death do the damned receive a "new body"? If so, why? The only reason would seem to be in order that they may be punished. But would it not be far more merciful to let them sink into total dissolution after death? Again, it may be asked how this state of "eternal sin" is transferred from the old body to the new? How can we speak of an eternal adherence to evil if consciousness consists only in successive psychic states without a permanent principle?

Heaven, too, is given very little attention. Nowhere is there indication that it consists in the beatific vision, in the possession of God through knowledge and love throughout eternity. Rather, it is suggested that eternal life is to be found right here on earth. Its nature, it is said, consists in a man's continuing influence for good. This is expressed in the following passage:

"May we not look further into revelation, to find the purest possible expression of how the new life is to be thought of, how we are to picture those dear to us who have died? If we do try, we find that revelation does not lead us away to a distant other-world. It points to our own. What, after all, is the greatest manifestation of the fulfillment of God's promises to us? It is the Easter apparitions of Jesus and His presence among us. We are shown how He is a friend who strengthens and consoles, and that He has remained the same ever since in the life of man-

— 167 —

kind, giving new force and peace, new gentleness and love. This manifestation—the permanent influence of the risen Lord since the first Easter apparition—is the purest indication that we have about the nature of eternal life, including that of those who have already fallen asleep in Him. To find out something about the new life of one who has died, we may fix our attention on the good which lives after him on earth.

"This rather than any nebulous fantasies, will help us to sense what eternal life is: man's fulfillment through dedication and love" (p. 474).

This passage can be read in a sense that is compatible with Christian revelation. However, one can also read in it the philosophy of Heidegger, which declares that man's only immortality consists in the influence for good he has left behind him on earth. If this is the true meaning of the passage, we are back to the doctrine of "courageous despair."

In fact, in reading various passages of the *Dutch Catechism,* one has a nagging impression that, underlying the Catholic phrases, there is a religious philosophy which is closer to that of Rudolf Bultmann than to Vatican II.

Discussion Points

1. What explanation does the *Dutch Catechism* give with regard to the origin of man, particularly of the human soul? What does it mean by saying: "Creation is a reality which strives upward," and "body and soul are not to be divided"?

2. Does this explanation leave any room for the spirituality of the soul of man? Why is this question so important? Could an animal, for instance, receive supernatural life, a share in the life of God? Why not?

3. Explain the traditional Christian distinction between matter and spirit. What are the activities of a spiritual being? Can it exist apart from matter?

4. What underlying philosophy makes the *Dutch Catechism* hostile to the spirituality of the human soul?

5. Summarize the attitude of the *Dutch Catechism* with regard to personal immortality. Do the authors conceive death as the total extinction of man, of his consciousness as well as his body?

6. How do they attempt to reconcile this doctrine with Christ's promise of eternal life? What was the concept of the ancient Jews with regard to life after death?

7. Answer the objection that it is "unbiblical" to picture the spirit of man as surviving the dissolution of his body.

8. Discuss the attitude of the *Dutch Catechism* with regard to the final destiny of man. What difficulties can you point out with regard to its explanation of hell?

9. What picture does the *Dutch Catechism* present of the nature of eternal life? Does this description leave any room for conscious personal immortality? Can this description be reconciled with the concept of supernatural life presented in the New Testament and taught through the ages by the Church?

10. What's your final impression? Is the *Dutch Catechism* teaching the Christian doctrine of personal resurrection, or is it teaching in a veiled way the doctrine: "Make this a better world; for it is the only one you will ever have"?

CHAPTER XVI

THE MOMENT OF TRUTH

The climax of a bullfight is called "the moment of truth." The fierce charges of the bull and the graceful passes of the matador are ended. Now man and beast stand facing each other, almost "eyeball to eyeball." The only way the man can move in for the kill is to dive with his sword straight between those powerful, pointed horns. Whatever one personally thinks of the sport, he must admit that this is a moment which puts a man to a supreme test of courage.

When one is confronted with the mystery of Christ and His Church, he arrives at a similar moment of truth. However much he may be convinced of the credibility of Christian doctrine, however strong be the movement of grace, when a man makes an act of faith, he is taking a "leap in the dark." He is accepting on the word of God an interpretation of life whose truth he himself cannot directly perceive nor completely understand. He is surrendering the deepest areas of his being, the convictions of his mind and the love of his heart, because he is convinced of God's truthfulness and goodness.

The act of faith is a response to God's revelation of himself given to us through Jesus Christ, His Incarnate Son. This Christian revelation, proclaimed by the apostles and written in the Scriptures, is presented to us through the living voice of the Church. The Church is the guardian and interpreter of divine revelation.

CONTENT OF REVELATION

When we consider the content of divine revelation, three important questions arise: 1) Is divine revelation absolute and unchanging in its essential message, or does its content change from age to age? 2) To what extent can the outward expression of this divine revelation change to meet the circumstances of different cultures and of different times? 3) Who makes the final decision whether a change in expression also involves a change in essential doctrine?

Again we will center our attention around the *Dutch Catechism,* since this book has been accused by some of religious relativism, and of changing both the expression and the meaning of important Catholic doctrines.

ABSOLUTE AND RELATIVE TRUTH

Let's start with the central problem of whether man can attain to absolute truth with regard to religion. Of course, there are many problems to which we simply do not know the answer. But are there any absolute and unchanging truths which have been revealed to us by God? Can the mind of man attain to certitude with regard to such truths?

The answer which a person gives to this question will depend upon his attitude toward the still deeper question of whether the mind of man can know objective truth at all.

1) Some say that man can never be certain of anything outside his own mind, and that, therefore all truth, including that of religion, is relative.

2) Others, while accepting the subjectivist position that man cannot be certain of anything outside his mind, postulate an immediate and direct revelation by God to the individual. In such a case, they hold, man can have the certitude of faith. However, it must be pointed out, such a faith would be purely personal and subjective, since it is based neither on the Bible nor the teaching of the Church.

3) The traditional Catholic position is that God has given an objective revelation of himself through His

Son, Jesus Christ. This revelation is accompanied by sufficient signs of its divine origin and credibility. A man who makes the act of faith, moved by grace, can have absolute certitude with regard to the truths which God has revealed. The content of divine revelation is unchanging, although we can penetrate its meaning more deeply, and express it in terms suitable to the age in which we live.

What does the *Dutch Catechism* say about this matter? It begins by declaring the unchanging nature of God's message and the infallibility of the Church regarding the truth of Christ. (p. 365) However, it goes on to explain:

> "In the past, infallibility was undoubtedly regarded too much like a cash-book: it was entered or not, and that was the end of it. Truth was regarded as a rock, and if it was not a rock, it could not remain faithful to itself. Too little attention was paid to the fact that we never deal with the truth as such, but only with the expression of the truth. The same truth must always be said in new ways and adapted to new conditions if it is not to grow stale and wither.

> "Modern conditions of life and thought have made it still more evident. But the result has been that some people have lost all sense of direction. Something that they thought was fixed now seems movable: the expression and adaptation of the truth. And they cannot recognize the unchanging and absolute nature of God's message in such movement" (p. 366).

The catechism goes on to explain that a fixed point need not be an immovable point. It uses the illustration of a mother who, though living and moving, is the fixed point for her child. However, the correctness of this example can be questioned. The mother is a fixed point for her child not in the literal sense, but only in the metaphorical sense that he depends on her for love and care. But it would involve a contradiction to say that a point can be fixed and moving at the same time and under the same aspect.

The question is: Does the *Dutch Catechism* merely change the expression of Catholic doctrine, or does it change the content of the doctrine? It is not enough to say the truth must be expressed in new ways to meet new conditions. We must take care that the new way of saying things actually expresses, and does not change, deny or cast in doubt the old, unchanging truth.

What does the catechism mean when it says that we never deal with the truth as such, but only with the expression of the truth? (p. 366) On the face of it, this statement seems to adopt the relativist position that man can never know truth as it is in itself, but only as it appears to him.

THE EUCHARIST

We have mentioned several times in this book how certain types of existential philosophers tend to consider things not as they are in themselves, but as they are in relation to man. This seems to be the approach adopted by the *Dutch Catechism* with reference to the real presence of Christ in the Eucharist. The catechism begins its explanation with this statement:

"When we consider the matter in terms of present day thought one should therefore say that the reality, the nature of material things is what they are— each in its own way—for man." (p. 343)

Here a realist would object that it is only because things have their own definite natures with determined properties that they can be used by man. For instance, it is only because mercury expands and contracts in response to heat and cold, that it can be used in a thermometer. It is only because steel is hard and can be sharpened to a point that man can use it to make a knife. It is only because some metals are extremely resistant to heat that they can be used in a rocket engine. It is pure relativism to say that it is the nature of things to be not what they are in themselves, but what they are for man.

The *Dutch Catechism* goes on to say:

"It is the essence or nature of bread to be earthly food for man. In the bread at Mass, however, this nature becomes something quite different: Jesus' body as food for eternal life."

When this statement is examined carefully, it seems to say not that the physical reality of bread has changed into the body of Christ, but that the relationship, or "meaning" of bread has changed. From being food for man's earthly life, it becomes food for eternal life. The essence of bread, it is said, consists in its relationship to man. Hence, when there is a change in this relationship, there is a change of essence. But is this explanation adequate to safeguard the real presence of Jesus Christ in the Eucharist? How can a relationship become the body of Christ?

Traditional Catholic doctrine, reaffirmed by Paul VI in his recent encyclical, *The Mystery of Faith,* has always taught that the whole physical reality under the appearance of bread becomes the body of Christ, and the whole physical reality under the appearance of wine becomes the blood of Christ.

That there must be such a physical reality is evident. Bread for the Eucharist is made from wheat; wine, from the juice of the grape. You can't make bread from iron, nor wine from sulphuric acid. However, in the explanation given by the *Dutch Catechism,* the underlying physical reality beneath the appearances of bread and wine seems to remain and to be merely given a new meaning, or significance.

The particular type of existential philosophy adopted by the authors of the *Dutch Catechism* has no room for the concept of essence, or substance, or nature, as a permanent reality under the appearances of things. The reason is that the essence, or substance of things can be known not by the senses, but only by the intelligence.

It is, however, contrary to the subjective and relative bent of mind of the authors of the catechism to admit that intellectual principles have validity outside the mind of man. Hence they are forced into the position that the nature, or essence of things is what they are for man. Logically, then, they must conclude that it is not the physical reality of bread and wine which is changed, but their essence is this relative sense, that is, their meaning or significance for man.

We can point out, too, that the underlying philosophy of the *Dutch Catechism* leads it to identify "body" with "person."

The words "this is my body" would then signify, "this is my person." "I am giving you myself."

But this misses the symbolism of the separate consecration of the bread and wine, of the body and blood of Christ. The Jews believed that the life of a living being was in its blood. Hence, for them, to separate the blood from the body was to cause it to die. We speak in a similar way today. Thus a soldier is said to "shed his blood for his country." To bring out this idea of the death of Christ, the words of the consecration of the wine clearly state: "This is my blood . . . which will be shed for you and for many unto the remission of sins." Missing this symbolism of the death of Christ leads one to over-emphasize the Mass as a meal and to under-emphasize it as a sacrifice.

THE NATURE OF GOD

As we examine the *Dutch Catechism,* we can perceive how its underlying philosophy is the reason for many of the positions which it adopts. For instance, you will read in its pages very little about the nature of God as He is in himself, or about His divine attributes. For the catechism is interested only in presenting God in His relationship to man, in His dynamic intervention in human affairs through salvation history. It even goes so far as to say: "We only know who God is through Jesus" (p. 79).

There may be a sense in which this statement can be rightly explained: but in its obvious meaning it is incorrect. We can know something about the nature of God, first of all, through creation. St. Paul declared: "Since the creation of the world His invisible attributes are clearly seen—His everlasting power also and divinity—being understood through the things that are made" (Rom. 1:20).

We can also know many things about the nature of God from the pages of the Old Testament. There is, for instance, the magnificent description of God as Creator and Lord of the universe in the book of Job (c. 38-39).

The psalms, too, speak in many passages about the attributes of God—His power, His wisdom, His goodness, His eternity and immensity. "The heavens declare the glory of God" (Ps. 18:1). "A thousand years in your sight are as yesterday" (Ps. 89:4).

Of course, Jesus completed and perfected man's knowledge of God. In doing so, He not only spoke of God's relationship to man, but also about God's relationship to the world outside of man. Christ tells us that God existed before the world began (John 17:5). He makes the sun to shine and the rain to fall (Matt. 5:45). He watches over the birds of the air and the lilies of the field (Matt. 6:26).

Only when we contemplate the infinite greatness of God in himself do we begin to comprehend in some small degree His love and mercy in the Incarnation. This was vividly expressed by St. Paul: "He emptied himself, taking the nature of a slave" (Phil. 2:7). It is important to emphasize the humanity of Jesus Christ; but it is equally important not to lose sight of His divinity. Excessive concentration on the "anthropological," on what God means to man, can lead to the secularizing of Christianity, the transforming of religion into sociology, and eventually to the "death of God" theology.

We do not mean that the authors of the *Dutch Catechism* in any way accept such extreme ideas. However, the type of philosophical thinking to which they subscribe has led others to such conclusions. It is not enough to have faith. One must also possess a philosophy which is in harmony with that faith. Descartes and Kant, for example, were both devout Christians. However, their subjectivism was incompatible with the Christian view of the world. Consequently, many of their followers drew the logical conclusion and dispensed with Christian belief altogether.

We could continue an analysis of the *Dutch Catechism,* showing how its at least partial acceptance of subjectivism and relativism gets it into difficulty with traditional theology and at times even with the official expression of revealed doctrine. However, enough has been written, we believe, to establish our central thesis. This can be summarized in the following statements:

SUMMARY

1) The confusion and anguish which affect many in the Church today result chiefly from the conflict of two philosophies, or mental attitudes.

The first of these attitudes is objective. It accepts as its basis the proposition that man can attain to objective truth about the world outside his mind. This philosophy emphasizes the essential, permanent, universal aspects of reality. It looks upon the world as created by the intelligence of God and as reflecting that intelligence by the ordered behavior of its parts. It stresses the objective character of divine revelation and the mission of the Church to teach, to guide and to sanctify mankind in accordance with the plan of salvation which God has revealed to us through Christ.

The second attitude is personalist and existential. It takes as its starting point the consciousness of man. It stresses the singular, unique, concrete, changing character of human existence. It is concerned with religion as a human experience, with man's right to grow according to his conscience, under the influence of grace, free from external coercion.

2) There is no essential contradiction between the objective and subjective viewpoint. Both assert positive values which must be incorporated into a mature overall view of total reality. There is a world external to man, of which he is a part, and to which and to whose laws he is subject. There is also the personal world of the consciousness of man. Both are real and true. The error comes when either view denies or disregards the other.

3) Historically, Catholic theology in recent centuries has been developed under the influence of Aristotelian philosophy, as applied to Christian revelation by St. Thomas and the scholastics. The Catholic faith, however, is not tied down to any particular philosophy. Nevertheless, since it is based on the fact of an objective divine revelation and the establishment by Christ of a Church to preach this revelation to mankind, it is incompatible with *subjectivism,* which denies the ability of the mind of man to attain objective truth.

4) Personalist, or existential philosophy, as a matter of fact, has developed under the influence of subjectivism. The application of this approach to Chris-

tianity has been made chiefly by liberal Protestant theologians in Germany and France. Many of them present religion as an affective, internal experience, which emphasizes the individual's search to be his "authentic self" and his concern for the welfare of others.

The influence of the subjective approach to religion made itself felt at Vatican Council II through the work of certain European bishops and their theologians. The Council accepted the positive values presented by personalism and began the process of harmonizing such values with traditional Catholic teaching.

5) Unfortunately, however, a number of Catholic theologians, Scripture scholars and popular writers have failed to distinguish the true and authentic values presented in the personalist approach from the erroneous philosophy of subjectivism with which these values were combined in the writings of such men as Heidegger, Bultmann and Tillich. The basic error of this religious subjectivism consists in its denial that the mind of man can attain objective truth and its assertion that all statements about religion are purely relative and subject to change.

ROCK OF REFUGE

At this point, the average Catholic may be tempted to throw up his hands in despair and cry out: "How, then, am I to discover the truth? I don't have a sufficient background of knowledge to detect what is correct and incorrect in the religious controversies swirling around me. If even some Catholic theologians, priests and nuns are getting off the right track, how am I to find the way to truth for myself and my children?"

The answer is very simple and very clear: "Listen to the teaching authority of the Church!" And this means to the Pope and to the bishops. They alone are the official teachers of the Church. They alone are the successors of the apostles to whom the commission was given to go forth and teach in Christ's name.

CHURCH WITH AUTHORITY

If there is anything clear in the New Testament, it is that Christ gave to His Church *authority*. He said: "As the Father has sent me, I also send you" (John 20:21). "Even as thou hast sent me into the world, so I also have sent them into the world" (John 17:18). So he who hears you, hears me; and he who rejects you, rejects me" (Luke 10:16). "If he refuse to hear even the Church, let him be to thee as the heathen and the publican" (Matt. 18:17). "Whatever you bind on earth shall be bound also in heaven; and whatever you loose on earth shall be loosed also in heaven" (Matt. 18:18).

This power to teach, to govern and to sanctify mankind, the Church claimed and exercised from the beginning of her history. When a dispute arose as to whether the first gentile Christians were obliged to observe the law of Moses, the apostles assembled the first council of Jerusalem. After deliberation, they wrote: "For the Holy Spirit and we have decided to lay no further burden upon you but this indispensable one, that you abstain from things sacrificed to idols and from blood and from what is strangled and from immorality" (Acts 15:28).

Throughout the Epistles of Peter, Paul, James and John, this same note of authority is evident. St. Paul, for example, writes: "We have received the grace of apostleship to bring about obedience to faith among all the nations for his name's sake" (Rom. 1:5). In correcting the Corinthians: "What is your wish, shall I come to you with a rod, or in love, in the spirit of meekness?" (1 Cor. 4:21) He passes judgment on the man guilty of incest: "I . . . have already passed judgment in the name of our Lord on the one who has so acted" (1 Cor. 5:3).

As the Church spread throughout the world, it was organized even in the time of the apostles, under bishops and priests who were given the same authority to govern the Church in Christ's name. Thus St. Peter writes: "Now I exhort the presbyters . . . tend the flock of God which is among you, governing not under constraint, but willingly according to God. . . . Likewise you who are younger, be subject to the presbyters" (1 Pet. 5:1).

The early Fathers and writers of the Church, even in the first century, such as St. Clement of Rome, St. Ignatius of Antioch, and St. Polycarp, universally acknowledged the hierarchical structure of the Church in virtue of which the faithful were obedient to their pastors because of the authority transmitted to them by Christ through the apostles and their successors.

This is the self concept which the Church, under the guidance of the Holy Spirit, has developed of herself through the centuries. She recognizes herself as a visible body in which the members profess the same faith, receive the same sacraments, and are united under the authority of the pope and the bishops, as successors of St. Peter and the apostles.

SOURCE OF UNITY

The teaching authority of the Church is the source of her unity. Without it, everything would fall into chaos. It is quite clear from the multitude of religious opinions around us today that the infallible guidance of the Holy Spirit, which Christ promised to His Church, has not been given to individuals.

It has been given only to those who have the official mandate to teach in Christ's name. All others have the obligation of receiving this teaching: "He said to them, 'Go into the whole world and preach the gospel to every creature. He who believes and is baptized shall be saved, but he who does not believe shall be condemned' " (Mark 16:15).

The faithful Catholic knows that Christ, upon leaving the earth, established His Church, which He sent forth in His name with authority to teach, to govern and to sanctify all mankind until the end of time. In obedience to Christ's Church, he finds unity, security and the certainty of doing God's will. For Christ has said: "He that hears you hears me" (Luke 10:16).

Discussion Points

1. Why does faith necessarily include "a leap in the dark"? What is the object of man's act of faith?

2. Bring out the difference between private and public revelation. Is the content of public revelation unchanging? To what extent can the expression of this revelation change? How can one tell whether a change in expression involves also a change in essential doctrine?

3. Analyze the explanation which the *Dutch Catechism* gives of the real presence of Christ in the Eucharist. Why do the authors of the catechism dislike the term "transubstantiation"? In their explanation, is there a real change of the bread and wine into the body and blood of Christ? Or is there merely a change in meaning, or significance, with the bread and wine retaining the same physical reality? What has been the teaching of the Church through the ages on this matter?

4. Is it true that we can "only know who God is through Jesus"? Can we also know God through creation? Through the Old Testament?

5. Have you noticed in recent religious writings a concentration of attention on the "humanness" of Christ, with a lessening of attention to His divinity? What is the reason for this?

6. Summarize briefly the doctrine of this book. 1) Explain the difference between the objective and subjective viewpoint with regard to reality. 2) Show how both attitudes must be incorporated into a mature overall view of total reality. 3) Relate how the personalist approach to philosophy and theology entered the stream of Catholic thought at Vatican II. 4) Bring out the need to separate true personalist values from the philosophy of subjectivism and relativism with which they have been combined by some modern writers.

7. Where can the ordinary person find security and certainty amid the religious confusion that exists today? Explain Christ's commission to His Church to teach, to govern and to sanctify mankind.

8. What has been the Church's understanding and exercise of her authority in the centuries since Christ.

9. How do you explain the antagonism which certain Catholic writers have recently exhibited toward the teaching authority of the Church?

10. Need we, as Catholics, be blind to the human failings of those who hold authority in the Church? Do such failings excuse one from obedience to duly constituted authority?

11. Explain the duties of obedience, loyalty and love which each Catholic owes to the Church which is the Bride of Christ and the spiritual Mother of the souls of men.

NOTE:

Since the first printing of this book, the special Commission of Cardinals appointed to study the *Dutch Catechism* has issued a declaration.

While praising many laudable aspects of the *Catechism,* the Commission called for emendations on ten major points.

These include all the subjects mentioned in our last three chapters. The *Catechism* is to teach clearly and without ambiguity:

1) the Virgin birth of Christ;

2) the immediate creation of the human soul;

3) the existence of angels;

4) the traditional doctrine on original sin;

5) the satisfaction made by Christ for sin;

6) the sacrificial character of the Mass and the real change of bread and wine into the body and blood of Christ;

7) the infallibility of the Church in preserving and teaching revealed mysteries;

8) the hierarchical priesthood and the power of teaching and ruling in the Church;

9) the possibility of true miracles;

10) the existence of absolute moral laws and the indissolubility of Christian marriage.